TAKING DOWN GOLIATH

To Jami —

THANKS SO MUCH FOR ALL YOUR HELP!

CHEERS!

TAKING DOWN GOLIATH

DIGITAL MARKETING STRATEGIES FOR
BEATING COMPETITORS WITH 100
TIMES YOUR SPENDING POWER

KEVIN M. RYAN AND
ROB "SPIDER" GRAHAM

palgrave
macmillan

First published in 2014 by
PALGRAVE MACMILLAN®
in the United States—a division of St. Martin's Press LLC,
175 Fifth Avenue, New York, NY 10010.

Where this book is distributed in the UK, Europe and the rest of the world,
this is by Palgrave Macmillan, a division of Macmillan Publishers Limited,
registered in England, company number 785998, of Houndmills,
Basingstoke, Hampshire RG21 6XS.

Palgrave Macmillan is the global academic imprint of the above companies
and has companies and representatives throughout the world.

Palgrave® and Macmillan® are registered trademarks in the United States,
the United Kingdom, Europe and other countries.

ISBN: 978–1–137–44420–2

Library of Congress Cataloging-in-Publication Data is available from the
Library of Congress.

A catalogue record of the book is available from the British Library.

Design by Newgen Knowledge Works (P) Ltd., Chennai, India.

First edition: November 2014

10 9 8 7 6 5 4 3 2 1

Printed in the United States of America.

FOR THEM ALL

CONTENTS

FIGURES

FOREWORD

WHY SMALL IS BEAUTIFUL

A core maxim of business journalism is "follow the money." At *Advertising Age*, that means tracking the multinational conglomerates, the P&Gs, Verizons, and General Motors of the world as they funnel ad budgets through giant agency holding company structures to the biggest ad sellers of the world, the likes of which today are Google, The Walt Disney Company, and Time Warner.

Once, that triumvirate—the marketer, the agency, and the media company—was dominant by dint of their size. The more ad spending you have, the more leverage you can wield in the marketplace. The world was simple. Everyone knew his or her place. Success was measured in tiny percentage increments each year. Disruption, when it happened, came over decades; gradually once-dominant brands, such as Sony and Blockbuster, started to decay and were soon replaced after shifts in technology or market conditions.

Well, I'm here to tell you that that time has ended. Actually, it ended some time ago, but it's only now starting to become obvious. If you just follow the money today, you'll miss the next big story, the one that's right under our noses. That's the story of how thousands of challenger brands—largely small and mid-sized companies—are using technology to transform markets and upend the status quo.

Big marketers of the past leveraged scarcity—a limited number of TV spots in prime time or shelf space at grocery stories—to protect their position. That worked when people were watching four networks and shopped in brick-and-mortar stores. Today, they're glancing at their smartphones thousands of times a day. Attention has fundamentally shifted and splintered. The first generation raised on touch screens and YouTube is in middle school today. Ask these people if they watch things on "broadcast" or "cable" TV, and they will look at you with a mixture of confusion and pity.

The disaggregation of attention is a fundamental threat to established brands and a huge opportunity for small and medium-sized upstarts. No one sells more coffee in grocery stores than Nescafé, but you'd never know that from Amazon.com where you'd think the world drinks Green Mountain Coffee out of K-cups. Similarly, you won't find an ad for Red Bull on TV, but Red Bull's "Stratos" stunt, where Felix Baumgartner jumped from the edge of space, has been viewed more than 200 million times—a couple Super Bowls for anyone who's counting. Similarly, a brand like GoPro can ascend based largely on videos shot by its users.

Big marketers are no longer looking around at their big, legacy competition; what's really giving them heartburn are the upstarts, the small and mid-sized brands that could become dominant tomorrow.

Here's how the small brands become dangerous. First, they take risks. Small brands that took a chance in social media reaped huge rewards on Facebook and Twitter. They know their audience and how it is using technology. That might mean understanding a new generation of messaging apps that are replacing Facebook in the hearts—and on the home screens—of young people. Small brands move fast and experiment—first. A theoretical understanding of new platforms won't do; you have to be first to understand. That means knowing the culture and your brands' value within it. Small brands challenge every orthodoxy. That may be the biggest opportunity for a small brand. While giant marketers tweak their plans here and there, small brands aren't beholden to tradition; they can pivot fast and jump on opportunities as they present themselves.

None of this, by the way, is easy. Easy was having the most money. It is much harder to figure out how to leverage limited resources across many different platforms and consumer touch points. And it is harder still to measure those investments and adjusting them on the fly, often in real time.

But the truth is that there's never been a better time to be a small brand. With the right foundational knowledge, a budget, and some savvy, a small brand can punch way above its weight. But how to get there? Schools are at least a decade behind and so are most marketing departments and agencies. That's where the authors, Kevin Ryan and Spider Graham, come in.

There are two kinds of people writing books about marketing today: those who make a living talking and writing about marketing (you can put me in that category) and those who actually do it. Kevin and Spider aren't part of the pundit class; they're too busy making small and mid-sized brands look and act big. These guys love what they do and have provided invaluable insights to me over the years.

What follows is an advanced education in what works today. It's a how-to for the next generation of dominant brands; the next story in American business.

MICHAEL LEARMONTH
Global Tech Editor at *International Business Times*
Former Deputy Managing Editor at *Advertising Age*

INTRODUCTION

Welcome to the digital advertising revolution. We saved you a seat.

One of the interesting things about being in the middle of a major paradigm shift is that major changes seem to happen so gradually that it sometimes feels like the world we live in today has always been this way.

When we look back just a few years, we see a world without many of the tools and technologies we now depend on every day: smartphones, search engines, tablets, video on demand, social media channels like Facebook, LinkedIn, Twitter, YouTube, and the Internet in general! These tools and channels have forever changed our lives and have also changed how we look at the world as both consumers and marketers.

Advancements in software, auction-based media, analytics, and big data have made it possible for the average marketer to compete with marketers with 100 times the spending power. Success in marketing is no longer the domain of companies who have deep pockets and extra marketing muscle. Instead, any marketer who understands how to navigate the challenges of this realm is able to make an impact that will draw the attention of the right people. In fact, today many of these Goliath marketers are at a disadvantage because the marketing models they've employed for many years no longer work.

In the past, big brands got all the attention and the highest priced agency talent, and the marketing middle-class masses got left out in the cold without the big budgets for media and agency talent. Today, marketers in this no man's land have a better chance than ever for success. The playing field has been leveled. The cost of admission has been dropped dramatically, and success goes to those advertisers who understand how to leverage what they have. Advertising success is no longer about having the biggest budget, and it's certainly no longer about reaching the greatest number of people as often as possible.

The digital universe has dramatically changed how marketers communicate with their prospects and customers. However, despite the advantages that automated digital media planning, buying, and distribution systems bring, the underlying strategies are what make them work. In short, effective digital advertising goes far beyond just placing an ad banner on a web page.

David has never had a better chance at beating Goliath, but digital marketing remains a mystery to the vast majority of would-be marketers. In other words, marketing automation and supposed turnkey systems will only get you so far, you still need a solid strategy.

Whether you run a big company or are a one-person marketing department, the digital marketing universe offers an incredible opportunity for marketers and advertisers of all types to finally create and execute campaigns that can be perfectly targeted, executed, and measured for success.

Taking Down Goliath is about learning how to approach the strategies and tactics needed to successfully navigate digital advertising. While we share insights into ways to design and create effective digital advertising campaigns, this is not a how-to book about specific creative or campaign considerations. Instead, our goal has been to share with you digital advertising business realities that will clear a path in the jungle before you so that you can eventually find your way to your goals.

During our time together we will serve as your guides to show you how to think about online advertising and marketing campaigns, and we will look at each marketing discipline in detail so you will learn what to do, where to look, how to execute, and most of all, **what to avoid**.

We have spent years working closely with advertisers offering them strategic digital marketing guidance and helping them to effectively start online conversations with the people they most need to talk with. Along the way we've learned four very important things that stand as pillars of success in digital marketing and advertising:

1. *All* successful advertising campaigns start by getting the right message to the right person at the right time.
2. *All* successful advertising campaigns are based on solid campaign planning, goal setting, audience targeting, and meaningful measurement of campaign results.
3. There is absolutely nothing magical about digital advertising channels and technologies. They are just tools and each offers marketers different strengths and weaknesses.
4. Effective online advertising isn't about how much money you have to spend. It's about how well you spend the money you have.

Really. It's that simple.

Yet, for years we've seen more advertisers than we can count create one-size-fits-all ad campaigns and place them where they don't talk to the right people. We've seen a multitude of advertisers spend thousands and thousands of dollars running digital ad campaigns without having bothered to spend a cent to measure campaign effectiveness or return on investment. We've watched advertisers spend gobs of money on embracing new technologies and marketing channels that don't even come close to meeting the needs of their prospects and consumers.

In short, we've seen plenty of bad advertising practices that do little more than spend the advertiser's money.

On the other hand, we've also seen small businesses with very limited resources create phenomenally successful online advertising campaigns because they first took time to think about what they were trying to accomplish and how they were going to measure whether what they were doing worked or not. We've seen small and medium-sized businesses create impactful ways to start meaningful conversations with the people they most want to talk to. We've seen marketers who understand that basically the consumers they most want to reach are people just like themselves.

Taking Down Goliath was written so that we could share with our readers the best digital advertising campaign planning practices known today. Throughout this book we will explore together the sound digital marketing strategies we've learned along the way and ways marketers can work toward effective and actionable campaign results.

We will explore different digital media channels and outline best practices for each and give readers the understanding they can apply toward their own campaigns. We'll also combine case studies from digital brands that emerged using the tactical outlay and overarching strategies that their Goliath competitors couldn't see coming.

HOW TO USE THIS BOOK

Through this book we have shared our experiences and strategies for how to create effective and actionable digital advertising campaigns. Our goal is to help you to avoid pitfalls that we learned about the hard way and to quickly tame and take advantage of the most incredible marketing channels that have ever been created.

We both believe fervently that every campaign is unique and that it's very difficult to create any kind of recipe that when followed will lead to campaign success. However, we also believe that there are best practices that should be followed whenever possible.

It may surprise you that the most important aspects of digital advertising have little to do with the digital channels that deliver ads. While we won't deny their importance, the most important aspects of any campaign are the steps taken before an ad campaign ever gets off the drawing board. In short, it has been our experience that campaign success is *always* driven by paying attention to the fundamentals of any good marketing approach including:

- Knowing what you're trying to accomplish
- Knowing what you want to say
- Knowing who you want to say it to
- Measuring whether what you wanted to have happen happened

Once you've nailed down these four areas of understanding, the rest of the campaign will often take care of itself.

The bulk of this book explores the different marketing channels that digital advertising is using today. We encourage you to jump to any chapter that you feel will best meet your needs and start there. However, we also encourage you to read the first four chapters of this book so that when you arrive at the channels, you will already have a great understanding of campaign goal setting, message creation for interactive environments, accurately defining target audiences, and understanding how to measure campaign success. You'll be glad you did.

HOW NOT TO USE THIS BOOK

We didn't write this book because we expect to make a billion dollars. We're not here to idealize and therefore encourage more upper-middle-class young people to throw away their higher education in favor of what has become the digital marketing pipe dream—forget the establishment, thumb your nose at the rules, and you'll make billions.

Let's not forget the world's largest social connecting device started because some kid couldn't figure out how to communicate with the opposite sex in any sort of meaningful way. Sure, really brilliant people struggle with formal education, but what gets a lot less press coverage is what happens to the majority of wannabe billionaires who don't learn any of the rules before heading out to break them all. Those guys spend an awful lot of time with jobs requiring hair nets and name tags. Let's face it: if everyone was that good, there would be a lot more ghostwritten feel-good books explaining how leaning in one direction would lead to a better life.

We're not here to sell you mystical ideas about how to change the way you measure by building elaborate mathematical glasshouses. We know you're a good person who needs to get things done, and simply building a good career, making a good living, having a meaningful life balance, and making a contribution to the world is all you're really looking for.

Most of the folks using this book don't get access to the latest stuff because they aren't spending enough to get attention. Most of the people reading this book aren't on big corporate boondoggles paid for by ridiculously large advertising budgets worthy of courtship by vendors who can afford such things. You are most likely in the middle tier of marketing—the vast and diverse middle class–left to navigate the world on your own.

In the past, big brands got all the attention and highest priced agency talent, and the marketing middle-class masses got left out in the cold without the big budgets for media and agency talent. Today, marketers in this middle ground have a better chance than ever for success.

We've had junkets, enjoyed many a night of fine dining and other stuff not worth discussing. At least one of us is embarrassed to say he expected such things as part of his compensation at one point. More important than the boondoggles and lunches are the access points to new and better technologies and talents being offered only to the top tier. It's a vicious cycle that rewards only a precious few in spite of the fairy tales about stock options and wealth for all.

We've chosen to bring balance to the digital marketing economy by leveling the playing field in some small way. In a lot of ways, the digital marketing playing field has never been more level. Enormous advancements in software, auction-based media, analytics, and big data have made it possible for the average marketer to compete with marketers with 100 times the spending power.

We're not trying to sell you on things we haven't already done ourselves. We have worked (and continue to work) in the digital marketing field since it began. We have volunteered our time, spent countless hours working to help build standards so that future generations of marketing professionals could work in our chosen field.

We're not here to tell you which tools to select. We want you to know that the players on the field change so much that your approach to resource selection has to be a big part of your digital marketing strategy. You shouldn't depend on one channel for your success. You have to know how all the pieces of the puzzle work together to be successful. We hope with some of the case examples we've included you can see how entrepreneurs—through their successes, near misses, and sometimes failures—have built businesses and careers.

A solid business strategy has become a lost art. Technology has enabled us to a fault. And the fault lies in the silo-fication of marketing disciplines. Technology in the form of marketing automation, media buying management, and optimization only facilitates and enables, it doesn't create a strategic environment.

David has never had a better chance at beating Goliath, but digital marketing remains a mystery to the vast majority of marketers. In other words, marketing automation will only get you so far, you still need a solid strategy.

This is not a get-rich-quick scheme. The reason digital marketing remains a mystery to many marketers is the decided lack of information from qualified sources, namely, from people who actually do the work, not just self-declared experts.

There is no quick fix or silver bullet, and there is no secret formula. In order for you to compete with marketers with 100 times your spending power, you'll need discipline, resource commitment, and the courage to invest in strategy.

This book wasn't written for the big spenders, although if you happen to be working inside a silo in a big company, it wouldn't hurt you to learn about something other than what you do every day. Your jobs are not without their pitfalls—and we understand that—so whether you run a big company or a one-person marketing department, the digital marketing universe represents set of challenges unlike any other.

While we won't repeat overplayed case studies, this book will profile the strategies and tactics needed to successfully navigate digital marketing. It will explain each marketing discipline in detail: what to do, where to look, how to execute, and most of all, what to avoid.

You won't see the case studies about how billion dollar powerhouses used their influence to get people to eat more cookies while watching football. You will see examples of entrepreneurs and middle marketers who not only survive but create winning environments using the tactical outlay and overarching strategies that their Goliath competitors couldn't see coming.

Finally, while we appreciate the flood of digital marketing books written by people who have companies funding their writing efforts, we'd like you to know that no one is paying us to fly around the world to look smart at book signings. We work every day to manage our businesses and writing this book came at a price. In other words, we're not selling you anything we have not done and continue to do in our daily lives. We're just a couple of guys who were there in the beginning, hope to be there when digital marketing matures, and seek a life beyond that.

Now, let's move on to the meaningful parts.

CHAPTER 1

THE DIGITAL ADVERTISING BIG BANG

It's incredible how the simple idea of connecting computers together changed the behaviors of people all around the world.

The slow progression of the Internet came from very humble roots. Initially created as a defense initiative so that military minds around the world could quickly get on the same page at the same time, the Internet then evolved into a useful tool for the scientific community to be able to share research and ideas.

The first pass at bringing the Internet to the mainstream was limited by a UNIX-based operating system that very much mirrored early DOS and relied entirely upon a command line interface and on people knowing many arcane terms. It was not what you would have called user-friendly.

Then in late 1992, the National Center for Supercomputing Applications (NCSA) at the University of Illinois Urbana-Champaign released the first web browser (Mosaic) based on a graphic user interface (GUI) and ushered in the modern age of the World Wide Web.

For the first time in history, consumers armed with a personal computer and a modem could log into computer server locations and gain access to a web of computers around the world that was quickly being linked together. This ushered in a technological boom that spurred the growth of personal computers, modems, Internet service providers (ISPs), and led to the ability for anybody connected to the web to access and share information with anybody else.

Most early websites left a lot to be desired. In most cases, they represented little more than brochures for the companies that talked a lot about themselves and really didn't offer much reason to stick around or return to their sites. Because the bandwidth that the average consumer was working with was so narrow, the use of graphics on most early websites was kept to a bare minimum in order to make the page load quick and easy. As a result, most early websites contained plenty of text but not much eye candy.

Then in 1994 something truly revolutionary happened. The designers of the site hotwired.com placed a rectangular graphic at the top of one of their web pages as part of a promotional effort they were working on with AT&T. This graphic was basically a large button that when clicked on took the site visitor off to the AT&T website. It was the first web banner ad ever used and first appeared on hotwired.com in October 1994 (see figure 1.1).

While web developers had been able to attach links to graphics prior to that time, the seemingly simple act of doing so for commercial purposes was truly a remarkable breakthrough. Click-through rates for this first ad surpassed 30 percent. It's fair to say that the majority of those clicks were from people who had read about this incredible breakthrough and visited the hotwired.com site to check it out for themselves. The clicks were not necessarily from a contingent of consumers suddenly intrigued by what AT&T was offering. Still, it was an important milestone.

What this event also drove home was the understanding that web publishers were now in a position where they could start to monetize their sites

Figure 1.1　The first online ads were simple and effective

by working directly with advertisers looking to reach the "eyeballs" of the rapidly growing audiences who were flocking to the web.

It was a fairly simple formula: advertisers wanted to get their messages in front of consumers, and consumers were voluntarily visiting websites they found interesting. By taking advantage of this traffic, both advertisers and publishers could meet their business goals.

This new approach also allowed advertisers to step away from more traditional mass marketing models in which all consumers were subjected to the same ad at the same time regardless of their personal needs or interests.

The new development also meant that publishers, many of whom had created their web properties more as a labor of love than as part of any solid business practice, were able to start running their sites like real businesses; the publishers now had greater control over the quality and quantity of what they offered site visitors.

This new model also created a massive paradigm shift in how consumers were expected to interact with advertising. At that time, most consumers had grown accustomed to a diet of broadcast and print advertising. These ad models were created to push a common message toward as many people as possible as often as possible, and consumers were never expected to do anything with those ads other than see and remember them. This model was sometimes referred to as a lean-back advertising approach.

Now consumers were expected to get involved in the advertising process by interacting directly with ads. These new lean-forward advertising models were based on the idea that consumers were now in the driver's seat.

Unlike traditional broadcast or print models, in which a programmer or an editor was responsible for making the fundamental decisions over the content to be shared with consumers, the new web model allowed consumers to pick and choose the information they found most interesting and useful. This meant that consumers were totally free to create their own information paths based on what they wanted, and at the same time they could also avoid what they didn't want. And often what they didn't want included advertising.

And this has brought us to a very interesting place.

THE DIGITAL ADVERTISING UNIVERSE

Not long ago, effective marketing was based on reaching the most people with a message. Today it's about reaching the right people.

For years, marketers and advertisers focused on ways to attract consumers' attention so they could promote their brands and share a message. They then created ad units using common broadcast or print formats and then bought media to get those ads in front of as many people as possible. The success of a campaign was often based on how many people it could reach, and reaching a lot of people cost a lot of money.

For the Davids in the crowd, necessity was often the mother of innovation. Because smaller advertisers and businesses were unable to afford the mass communications channels in their markets, they relied instead on guerilla marketing approaches, such as printed flyers, direct mail, the yellow pages, and small classified ads to tell their stories. Their limited budgets forced them to be careful with how they used their limited resources and to be more selective in who they delivered their messages to.

Then the universe changed.

As digital marketing channels came into being, savvy marketers recognized that effective advertising was no longer based on reaching everybody but instead was driven by the need to reach the right people with the right message at the right time. Trying to reach everybody wasn't possible online because of the enormous number of new channels that were being created daily. Instead, to advertise effectively online meant first knowing who you wanted to talk to and then figuring out which web sites these people were most likely to visit.

Suddenly the advertiser with limited resources had the same opportunities for market exposure as the Goliath advertisers with deep pockets. Success was no longer based on how much money a marketer had to throw at the market; instead, the new media gave innovative marketers better ways to connect with individual consumers.

It also gave advertisers new ways to tell compelling and engaging stories to their prospects and customers in order to grab and hold their attention. It meant that to be successful advertisers needed to think differently about how to approach new ad channels and formats and how marketing worked within these new digital channels. Before long, businesses of all sizes were starting to explore this new realm and quickly learning that the secret of success in digital advertising has little to do with getting the same message to everybody.

Today, the level playing field is giving marketers of all sizes extraordinary marketing tools to work with. The time to market for many campaigns has shrunk from months and weeks to days and hours. The cost of participation has dropped from thousands of dollars to absolutely free in many cases. It's no longer a case of whoever has the most money owns the market. Today, it's about innovation, finesse, and understanding who you most need to talk to and what those people want to hear.

It's a brave new world.

EXPLORING THE DIGITAL ECOSYSTEM

The way that information flows online is very different from how it flowed in most traditional media.

Traditional media, such as television, radio, and print, are channels that offer only one-way information flow. The consumer is expected to access this information through a central and controlled source. Consumers are also expected to do very little with that information other than to see and remember it.

While there are direct response campaigns that rely on toll-free numbers or envelopes that need to be sealed and returned, the bulk of advertising through these traditional channels is about achieving a higher level of brand awareness. The channels tend to do that well because they are based on the idea of reaching as many people as possible as often as possible. This is a great formula for branding success.

But at the end of the day it's very difficult to measure the overall effectiveness of most traditional media channels. For example, when a TV spot runs, it's an easy task to measure what time it ran and on which channels. What's difficult to measure is the branding impact that the commercial had. How many people watched the commercial and what did they do with that information? Did they understand the value proposition? Was the message the consumer took away understood the way the advertiser intended it, and what did the advertiser really expect consumers to do with that understanding?

The reality of traditional advertising campaigns is that it's difficult to measure the impact of those ads because there are so many variables that need to be factored in. Even if advertisers could get an exact count of the number of consumers who watched a commercial all the way through, they would still not know which consumers found the ad relevant and meaningful.

We're not here to bash traditional media channels but to point out that they have limitations. Because these channels were never designed to be interactive (apart from the occasional direct response campaign), they generally lack meaningful feedback loops.

But the strength of traditional mass media marketing is also a large part of any successful online campaign. Today, most broadcast and print ads include features that drive traffic to online landing pages. Traditional publishers, such as the *Wall Street Journal* share lists of their most popular online articles in their newspaper. Magazines like *Bloomberg BusinessWeek* actively promote their online properties through print ads, and web sites like mentalfloss.com start creating printed magazines to extend their audience reach offline. The reality is that today's consumers aren't just sitting in one place. They are watching television both online and off. They read printed magazines and newspapers and also get information online. It's not either/or for how they find information or entertainment. It doesn't need to be either/or for advertisers either.

For a number of years, as digital advertising was cutting its teeth, a number of traditional agencies created ancillary digital agencies to help them take advantage of this new influx in advertiser needs. While this seemed to make sense on the surface, it quickly became a point of frustration for many advertisers because it created a totally separate campaign approach between broadcast and print campaigns and online campaigns. This disconnect not only created extra work for the advertisers, but it often meant that the campaigns that ran on traditional broadcast and print channels were completely different from those that ran online. It also meant in many cases advertisers had to go through different channels of media buying for each campaign.

Today, most agencies have figured out how to get the traditional and digital channels back under the same roof. In fact, most advertisers and agencies have learned how to take advantage of the interrelationship between the media channels. For example, most TV commercials today include a URL or link to a social media channel and are being used to drive additional traffic to these online properties. Print ads almost always include a URL that will lead readers to more information and special offers.

The bottom line is that a solid digital strategy often includes a traditional component. When it comes to beating Goliath, the secret is in how effectively you can communicate value and benefit.

THE ART OF ENGAGEMENT

If you can't get the attention of the people you most need to talk to, then nothing else you do in advertising matters. Period.

Getting the attention of people isn't easy. It's definitely not easy online mostly because there is already a lot of noise online vying for the attention of site visitors. But it goes deeper than that; even if you can get people to pay attention to you by doing something dramatic or even a little obnoxious (quivering banner ads anyone?), can you hold that attention?

Web site designers refer to it as making things sticky. The goal is to attract consumers' attention by giving them a fair value exchange—their attention in exchange for what the publisher or advertiser is offering. As you might imagine, value is very much in the eye of the beholder. Simply putting a banner ad on a web site is a far cry from creating an engaging experience for a consumer.

Instead, innovative marketers need to understand and address what it is that the people they most want to talk to are thinking about. They need to know how they can start a meaningful conversation with these people that allows them to address their needs and desires. They need to define and determine the best platforms and channels to use to communicate with these people. They need to figure out how to start a meaningful conversation with prospects and then move that conversation toward conversion over time. They have to know what that conversion looks like.

Despite all of the potentially moving parts that can be combined to achieve meaningful engagement in an advertising campaign, what really matters is that a meaningful exchange of understanding took place because the right consumers joined the conversation. This means that advertisers need to step away from thinking like an advertiser and start to think more like a friend.

Let's say you've just recently moved to a new city. After a few weeks, you make a new friend at the fitness center you've joined, and one day he invites you to a party at his home. While you're excited to go, you're also aware that the only person you will know at this party is the host and that everybody else will be a total stranger. Is this a problem? Should it be?

Fortunately, you possess good social skills, and so you approach the party as an opportunity to make even more new friends. After you arrive, you start to mingle. You eavesdrop on ongoing conversations to get a better sense of what conversations are taking place and where you might be able to add something to allow you to become part of that conversation. You might also be bold and walk up to a stranger and introduce yourself. Either way, you're able to assess the situation and look for ways you might start a conversation with people you don't yet know.

There are some strong similarities between how we engage and meet people at a party and how marketers need to go about "meeting" new customers. When we start a conversation with somebody we're meeting for the first time, we often begin by asking each other questions that allow us to get a better sense of what we have in common. We talk about where we live, what we do for a living, the weather, where we went to school, etc. We look for things that we have in common because that gives us a natural jumping-off point for continuing the conversation. As we go back and forth and reveal things about ourselves, our previous experiences, and our passions, we are able to expand the circle of commonality between us.

As we collect more data on one another we have more room to dig deeper. We share information about our families and our pets. We talk about things we experienced growing up. We talk about our philosophical and religious beliefs. We talk about things we are passionate about, things we collect, things we do in our free time. We talk about our favorite sports teams and restaurants we love to go to. We sometimes talk about how we feel about political issues and even some of the personal challenges that we have faced in our lives. We talk about very human things with other human beings. Over time we develop new relationships, create dear friends, and even find love and passion. But it first starts with being able to share the things that are most important to us.

Why did we suddenly jump into this philosophical exploration of the human psyche? Because, whether we acknowledge it or not, the people that we're trying to reach with our brands and services as marketers are the same people we could meet at a party. And the best way to meet them as consumers is to start by learning more about what makes them…them.

One of our main criticisms of advertising over the past 100 years is that Goliath advertisers rarely stop to consider the unique needs and perceptions of the individual people they are trying to reach. Instead, the advertisers made assumptions about what large groups want based upon a few data points. In most cases, advertising is relevant only to a very small percentage of any population at a given time. Not only that, most advertising campaigns offer only a single message that is rarely meaningful to everybody who comes in contact with it.

In fact, most traditional advertising is like going to a party and instead of taking time to better understand what conversations are taking place you, you just walk in the door, demand everybody's attention, and then launch into sharing your story without any care and consideration of what other conversations are already in progress.

Not only would this kind of behavior be incredibly antisocial and rude to most of the people at the party, but chances are good that your story, no matter how important to you, would be totally irrelevant in the context and would fail to make much of an impact. The odds are also pretty good that you would never be invited to another party!

Yet, most Goliath advertising campaigns still rely on mass marketing channels to saturate the market with their message. The marketers organizing those campaigns presume that it's okay to interrupt other people with their message. They presume that other people will automatically find their messages interesting and meaningful. They presume that people will stop and listen and care and like them. But in most cases this just isn't true.

We could argue that once upon a time mass marketing models worked. They accomplished the task of getting a brand message to as many people as possible so that those consumers could be self-selecting and use their new understanding to help them make an informed buying decision in the future. But we already know that only a small percentage of people are going to find *any* particular message personally relevant. Does it make sense to reach everybody when most people don't care and won't respond in a favorable way?

Another major challenge with most traditional advertising and marketing approaches is that they don't allow for continuity. For example, let's say that you go to a party and meet somebody by the punch bowl. You get in a conversation and start sharing basic information about yourselves, such as your names, where each of you live, what each does for living, which team you're rooting for during the upcoming Super Bowl, etc. In short, you look for points of commonality.

Because it's a party, you mingle with other guests. An hour later you bump into your new friend by the hors d'oeuvre table. Would you start the new conversation by asking him his name, where he lives, what he does for a living, and which football team he's rooting for during the upcoming Super Bowl? Chances are good that if you were to do that, he'd wonder if you're suffering from some sort of dementia!

Of course, you wouldn't start from scratch every single time you meet the same person because you already have a previous relationship. As ludicrous as this scenario sounds, this approach is very much how most traditional advertisers approach consumers every day. Because they are unable to measure previous contact with consumers and accurately know what was talked about, understood by the consumer, and because they don't know whether the consumer will ever become a customer of their product or service, most advertisers end up starting their conversations with consumers from scratch every time.

By contrast, the digital advertising universe offers marketers an incredible opportunity to change these models and make them more effective. We no longer have to rely on getting the same message out to everybody in the hope that the right people will be self-selecting. We no longer have to treat prospects and consumers like they are total strangers after we've already done business together. We no longer have to bombard people who just don't care about our products and services (and never will) with offers that are falling on deaf ears.

The digital universe offers advertisers a brave new world to work in where they can speak directly to the people who most want to hear what they have to say. It is a realm where advertisers can measure the impact of the marketing conversations that take place and use that understanding to drive the conversation forward. The digital universe works by allowing marketers to start personalized conversations with individual consumers that can be monitored for progress. It allows those conversations to be tailored as needed. Marketing is thus no longer a process based on interrupting consumers at every turn to scream at them that they should buy your products or services. Instead, we're reaching an age where listening carefully first can make all the difference in how we start and maintain future conversations with consumers.

UNDERSTANDING DIGITAL MARKETING FUNDAMENTALS

The ultimate goal of any advertising campaign is to raise awareness and drive consumers toward a point of conversion.

Again, this sounds like a fairly straightforward process because it is. What muddies up most campaigns is the lack of a clear definition of how to set goals, measure them to determine whether they're being met, and then fix anything that needs fixing.

When we think about ad campaign design, we look at it as a cycle during which each stage contributes to the overall effectiveness and success of the campaign. This optimization cycle generally consists of six distinct steps:

1. Set campaign goals/identify key performance indicators (KPIs)
2. Identify and reach target consumers
3. Define campaign message(s)
4. Determine campaign media channels
5. Measure campaign results
6. Optimize campaign approach/parameters

We will be covering each of these stages in much greater detail throughout this book, but for right now let's take a quick peek at the significance of each.

Set Campaign Goal/Identify Key Performance Indicators

We doubt that we have to explain to you the importance of setting clear and actionable goals for any campaign that you run. Still, we have had conversations with advertising clients too many times over the years in which we have asked about their campaign goals and objectives and have received answers along the lines of "That's a good question. I guess we'll figure it out as we go along."

Setting clear campaign goals is incredibly important for two distinct reasons. The first is that without knowing what you are trying to accomplish it's difficult to accomplish it. The second is that without having a clear target to aim at you have nothing to measure whether a campaign was successful or not.

It's also important that a campaign's goals mesh with the overall business goals. After all, if somebody were to ask you why you were spending time and money to push a campaign out the door, your answer should probably have something to do with having a goal of making that money back plus more. So the first question that needs to be answered is what are you trying to accomplish with your campaign and how do you intend to measure whether those goals are being met?

For example, let's say that an automotive manufacturer is running an online ad campaign. This campaign consists of a series of digital display ads (banner ads), and the advertiser is buying media on sites that cater to car buffs in general and truck drivers in particular.

We can probably guess accurately that the ultimate goal for this campaign is to drive traffic to dealerships so that interested prospects can go for a test drive. At the end of the day, the ultimate goal for the advertiser is to sell more trucks. And yet, it's entirely likely that the advertiser will spend the majority of the time and money involved trying to measure how many times the ads were clicked on. This isn't to say that measuring click-through rates doesn't have its place, but the challenges that many advertisers face is that what they can measure and what they should measure are different things.

We'll take a much closer look at campaign goal setting and analytics in Chapter 2.

Identifying Key Performance Indicators (KPIs)

A key performance indicator is basically something that can be measured and indicates whether the marketing or business goal is being achieved. For example, let's say that a retail store wants to measure the amount of foot traffic in the store on an average day. By putting a counting device in the doorway or even employing a person with a handheld counter to tally and tabulate foot traffic that number can be easily determined.

But let's say instead that the goal of the retailer is to determine how much money the store makes on an average day. While the number of people entering the store is certainly going to affect that number, simply measuring the traffic flow isn't going to provide any meaningful insight toward understanding how much money is being made. In this case, the retailer would have to look at the receipts from the day's sales to get that number.

Often the secret of success in advertising is based on first asking the right questions so that you can get the right answers. The same thing holds true for online advertisers. If the goal of the campaign is to acquire new customers, then the KPIs should focus on measuring those parts of the campaign (the number or people who willingly submitted an e-mail address on a campaign landing page, for example) to help determine whether new customers are being acquired. However, too often advertisers default to measuring click-through rates or something else that doesn't tell the right story, and they often don't consider what that is going to mean in the long run.

Identify and Reach Target Consumers

Let's state the obvious one more time: you have to know who you want to talk with before you can start having a conversation. It's not a particularly difficult task to identify the people who make up your best prospects and customers. You probably have a pretty good list of features that you already use to reach these people.

While the web allows us to focus on more clearly defined audiences and members, it's often more challenging to home in on individuals than on large groups. What criteria do we need to use to find these people? How do we best determine what they want and need?

When we target consumers online, one of the questions we need to be able to answer is what we want these consumers to do in response to seeing or interacting with our advertising? Furthermore, how will we measure those actions to determine whether consumers behaved the way we wanted them to?

Here's the bottom line with targeting customers: You're not going to do it perfectly the first time. You may know exactly the kinds of people that you need to talk to, but the odds are great that you're going to have to start off slowly and fine-tune your targeting over time.

Several years ago we worked on a campaign in which the client had done a thorough job of identifying who the target audience was. As a result, the media buy focused on reaching those people, and all of the campaign creative addressed the expected needs of this group.

When the campaign ran, there was only one minor problem: The people targeted by the campaign failed to show up or respond. Was the advertiser surprised? Absolutely. After all, the marketers knew definitively who their target customer was. But the problem was that they were wrong!

However, the good news was that while the target audience failed to show up, the marketers were able to measure and define a new audience. This was a new group of people who were paying attention to the advertising, visiting the website, and even buying the product—a group the advertiser had failed to notice before. But because the marketers measured the campaign results and looked at the characteristics of the people who were showing up, they were now able to target this new audience and optimize the targeting even further.

Define Campaign Message(s)

As we will explore in much greater detail in chapter 4, the message is an integral part of any effective marketing campaign. The message is basically the information, idea, thought, or understanding about a brand's products and services that needs to be delivered to a consumer. In short, after a consumer has seen, touched, interacted with, or experienced a marketing message then what is being left behind?

Messages can be simple branding messages that work to find a foothold in a consumer's mind so that the next time the individual sees that brand, it will seem familiar. Or they can be direct response approaches that request the consumer to do something specific to take advantage of an offer.

Determine Campaign Media Channels

The bulk of this book is about the different digital media channels available to marketers today along with best practices for their use and management.

Based on the goals of a campaign, the message of the campaign, and the audience being targeted, different media channels offer different strengths (and weaknesses) to a campaign. In most cases, multiple channels are used together during a campaign to create a richer and more effective communications approach.

Measuring Campaign Results

Ultimately, we want to know whether the campaign "worked." We can determine that only if we can accurately measure whether set goals are being met, whether previous campaign benchmarks were surpassed, and whether we are still asking the right questions to get the right answers.

A few years ago a British study concluded that 51 percent of the online digital display campaigns running at that time were not being measured in any way by advertisers. For those of us who've been in the trenches this seems like a squandered opportunity. Yes, the feedback that advertisers get from their campaigns can certainly be harsh from time to time. People don't enjoy finding out that they just spent a lot of money with very little to show for it. On the other hand, this feedback also serves to help advertisers understand where mistakes were made and how to avoid making those mistakes again.

The feedback also helps point out and reinforce things that advertisers are doing correctly. Without this feedback loop, marketers can only guess at the overall effectiveness of a campaign. While most of us truly want to believe that everything we put into motion is going to hit the bull's-eye dead center every time, the reality is that sometimes we don't even come close to hitting the target.

Measure, measure, and then measure some more.

Optimizing Campaign Approach

It has been our experience that regardless of how smart you are, how many resources you employ, and how carefully you plan a campaign, you are never ever going to hit the target dead center on the first try. So take a deep breath and be willing to make mistakes and then learn from those mistakes. The bottom line is that you can't improve what you don't measure.

Optimization of digital campaigns gives advertisers a rare opportunity to go and tweak the things that aren't working and reinforce the ones that are working and do so in real time. This is a welcome opportunity and something that most traditional advertisers could not hope to do. For example, a print ad running in a magazine that failed to elicit the desired consumer response can't be changed after the fact. The ad is going to sit on the page of that magazine forever. To fix a campaign that failed, the advertiser would need to go through a new creative process and submit a new ad to the publisher and go through the whole process again. However, with online media campaigns optimization is often a simple process of swapping out one ad for another. This doesn't affect the media buy, and it doesn't create any difficult trafficking problems, and the results of changes can be measured almost immediately.

The bottom line is that online advertising should never be a "set it and forget it" proposition. Every campaign needs to go through an evolution during which it gets better and better at what it was designed for.

THE FOUNDATIONAL COMMUNICATIONS MODEL

As marketers, we are in the business of persuasion. Our ultimate goal is to get people to change how they perceive their needs.

Regardless of what we sell and how we sell it, our ultimate goal is to get people to change how they see themselves in relation to our brands. Most successful marketers work to create meaningful relationships between their brands and services and the people they want to persuade. As we mentioned before, marketing is not a process of simply exposing consumers to a brand; it is a process of communicating values and benefits in a way that allows consumers to change how they perceive a brand or service. Not to sound too deeply philosophical, but one of the biggest challenges marketers face is figuring out ways to get consumers to change their behaviors and accept new ideas and outcomes.

At its core, marketing is about communicating with people. In fact, every marketing campaign since of the dawn of humanity has been fundamentally about finding the best ways to get the right message to the right person at the right time. While it seems like a straightforward objective, any experienced marketer can tell you that getting all of the elements of an effective campaign lined up is a bit like herding cats.

As complicated as marketing can be, every campaign starts with a basic approach:

1. Define the message to be delivered
2. Define the audience that message is intended for
3. Select a channel that can deliver that message to that audience

The foundational communications model shown in figure 1.2 is the basis for every effective mode of human communication and not just advertising.

For example, if you wanted to send your grandmother a birthday greeting, you might choose to buy her a card and write your best wishes inside the card (the message). Then using the postal service, you would address the outside of the envelope as required, affix the proper amount of postage, and drop the card in a mail box (the channel) so it can be delivered. If all goes well, a few days later your grandmother (the audience) will receive your best wishes.

As marketers and advertisers, we all have messages that we need to share with other people. The channels we use to deliver messages vary as does the

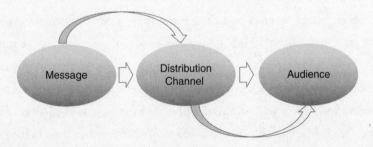

Figure 1.2 Foundational communications model

structure of the message. For example, instead of sending a card through the postal service, you could instead choose to send your grandmother an online e-card. Or perhaps you could create a short video of everybody in your family wishing her a happy birthday and then attach that video to an e-mail, or you might even create a YouTube channel and post your video there. There is more than one way to get the task accomplished.

However, effective communication is rarely about the channels we use to move the message. Instead, it's about creating content that is engaging and meaningful to its potential audience because it meshes with the audience's relevant needs, desires, intentions, and understanding. At its core, good marketing is about creating good relationships. It's about sharing understanding, stories, and news with prospects or customers so that a business can stay visible and viable. It's about maintaining market share and sustaining business continuity. Businesses that are unable to do these things effectively tend to stop being businesses.

Practical Wisdom—We often cringe a little when we hear some Goliath marketers talk about their customers in abstract terms such as "users," "visitors," and "buyers." While subtle, these terms have the tendency to distance marketers from the humanity of their customers, and thus these terms can get in the way of marketers communicating effectively with the people they most need to reach. Savvy marketers always keep in mind that it is these people who make a business a business. These marketers understand that they are communicating with real people who have distinct likes and dislikes, good days and bad. These are people who act rationally sometimes and irrationally at other times. These are people very much like the ones we see every morning in the bathroom mirror.

What does all this mean for small and medium-sized businesses? A lot actually.

While digital media channels often get a lot of buzz, the reality is that the channels we use to move messages across the marketplace are generally the least important part of the equation. Because there are so many different ways to communicate with consumers today, no single channel alone is going to do the trick, and effective digital campaigns generally require using multiple channels to meet campaign objectives.

One of the biggest challenges we face when working with advertising clients is the occasional need to help steer them away from "flavor or the day" technologies and channels that often have nothing to do with helping them achieve their marketing goals. This process sometimes sounds like this:

"So, what is it you're trying to accomplish? What are your campaign goals?"

"We want to have a Twitter campaign."

"Okay, we can certainly help you with that. But how will having a Twitter campaign help you achieve your overall campaign goals?"

"We would like to have a Twitter campaign so we can send tweets out to people."

"Okay, and do you know specifically which people you would like to reach with your Twitter campaign?"

"Yes, the people who will be receiving our tweets through our Twitter campaign."

After you bang your head against a wall for a while, you realize one of the main challenges that the whole digital industry faces is that there are plenty of marketers who believe that digital marketing and advertising is based on some sort of magic. The reality is that, like any other marketing channels and tools, digital advertising channels are ways to deliver messages to consumers; they're just newer. There is no magic wand that marketers can wave and suddenly all their marketing objectives fall into place in one fell swoop. There is no single tool or technology that will suddenly reach 100 percent of a target audience and generate so much money that managers will be swimming through huge piles of it in their foyers.

Digital marketing tools and channels are just that: tools and channels. Having access to them does not mean automatic success, just as owning a hammer does not make somebody a master carpenter. With any tool that is used on a regular basis the skills get stronger and that eventually translates into results, but it is by no means an automatic process.

The strategies that we share in his book are based on many years of experience and living through ad campaigns that run the gamut from being incredibly successful to being total failures. A huge part of any campaign's success is based on meeting the needs and expectations of consumers.

CHAPTER 2

SETTING AND MEASURING DIGITAL CAMPAIGN GOALS

If you don't know where you are going, any road will get you there, said Lewis Carroll. This goes for marketers too.

There's an old story about a guy who's out walking his dog one night when he sees another man walking around in circles underneath the streetlight and looking down at the ground. So the dog walker approaches him and says "Did you lose something, friend?"

"Yes," the other man replies. "I dropped my wallet!"

The dog walker joins in the search, and after combing the area very thoroughly and finding nothing says to the other man "There's no sign of your wallet. Are you sure you dropped it here?"

"No," the man replies. "I dropped it a few blocks up the street."

"What?" says the dog walker, shocked. "If that's the case, then why are you looking for it here?"

"Oh," the other man responds, "because the light's much better here!"

While this joke plays upon the absurdity of this type of thinking, too many online marketers and advertisers use a similar type of logic when measuring the overall effectiveness and success of their digital advertising campaigns.

As we discussed briefly in the preceding chapter, one cardinal sin of advertisers is to not bother to measure the results of their campaigns at all.

It happens more often than you might think. When we first looked at the percentage of advertisers who don't bother to measure campaign results a few years ago, the percentage was over 50 percent in some markets. Today, marketers are savvier, but the number of unmeasured digital campaigns is still disturbingly high. We think there are two primary reasons why marketers choose not to measure their campaigns:

1. They don't understand *how* to measure effectiveness and success of a campaign.
2. They don't want to measure campaign results in case the news is bad.

The first reason can be easily remedied by reading a book just like this one and learning what you need to know to do a better job. The second reason is a harder nut to crack.

Yes, it's a very human example of cover your butt. If you don't measure it, then your campaign can never be a failure, and therefore your job is safe—for now. As sad as this logic makes us, we get it. But we also see the bigger picture.

Advertising is a process. While we like to believe that everything we do is going to be a home run, the reality of advertising is that success is based on a consistent number of solid singles. We have both worked on campaigns that brought together some of the smartest and most creative minds around only to find that, despite good planning and creative excellence, the campaign still missed its mark. While this can be disheartening, we have found over time that getting anything right the first time is a very rare occurrence.

Practical Wisdom—Several years ago, a client discovered that the homepage for the company's website wasn't doing a very effective job moving site visitors to some of the other pages on the site, especially the ordering page. They had measured the flow of traffic from the previous six weeks and revealed that nearly 63 percent of site visitors weren't navigating past that first page.

So we pulled together a group of web designers, copywriters, and marketing managers and set about fixing the problem. A week or so later we had a newly redesigned landing page that was more robust, contained an introductory video, and overall did a much better job of explaining to site visitors the benefits and reasons why they should stick around and buy the product.

When the new page went live, we felt we had done the best job possible to fix the problem. But instead of giving each other high fives and heading out to grab a drink, we started measuring the results from our changes. Much to our disappointment, the results of the new metrics showed us that the changes we had so carefully thought about and put into place were resulting in nearly 90 percent of site visitors leaving the site after only the first page! Of course, we immediately pulled the new page down and went back to the old page as we reassessed our thinking.

Nobody sets out to do a bad job. As far as we knew, we had nailed this thing. But what we wanted and what we got were two different things. Fortunately, the feedback from digital campaigns can give us additional insights and understanding into the reasons why online consumers behave as they do.

Let's say that a friend invites you to join him at a shooting range one afternoon. You don't know much about guns, but your friend is patient and willing to guide you toward becoming a better marksman by covering the basics of posture and breathing and control of the weapon. As you stand with the weapon in your hands and line the rifle's sight up with the bull's-eye, everything looks like it's literally right on target. And then you pull the trigger.

So what happens next?

Your friend, who is using a spotting scope to watch your target, sees that your shot went low and to the left and that you just barely nicked the edge of the target. Does this mean that you failed horribly and that you should just give up immediately because it's obvious you will never be a proficient marksman? Of course not. Instead, because of the feedback you're receiving, you are able to make minor adjustments and try different approaches with each shot until you are able to hit the center of the bull's-eye almost every time.

Like shooting at targets, proficiency in advertising isn't about getting it right the first time. It's about knowing what to measure that will tell you how to do a better job next time. Through this measurement and analysis of campaign results we can create feedback loops that give us the insights we need to become more and more proficient at the task.

The reality of advertisers who don't bother to advertise because they fear that they may do it wrong is that they will also never create an opportunity to learn how to do it right.

SETTING REALISTIC CAMPAIGN GOALS

Setting advertising campaign goals is paramount; setting realistic campaign goals is even more so.

The reality is that just because you set a goal doesn't mean you're going to achieve it. What goal setting allows us to do is to set a destination we want to head toward. In marketing, setting realistic goals also gives us something possible to aim for.

When we set campaign goals we are in essence creating a road map. We're trying to visualize what the finish line looks like based upon what we want the campaign to accomplish. A quick checklist might include the following questions:

- What are the goals of the campaign?
- How do the individual ad units support those goals?
- How do the landing pages and other marketing materials support the goal?
- How will those goals be measured to determine success?

Setting and achieving advertising and marketing goals is often based upon experience. Understanding what the norms for an industry are is a good place to start.

Practical Wisdom—Several years ago a client was trying to create a direct response campaign to get consumers to come to a landing page so they can print out a brochure. When I pointed out to her that we could create ads that could meet the same goals without requiring any traffic to go to a landing page, she was intrigued. So we created an interactive ad that focused on encouraging consumers to click on a large button and then immediately print out the brochure to their own printer.

We designed the ads to make it clear to consumers that they could accomplish what they wanted to without having to leave the page they were on. No click-through required!

When the campaign went live, we gave it a few days to work its magic so that we could establish the baseline for how it was working. When I looked at the interaction rates for the ad a few days later, I was blown away. The interaction with the print button in the ad was surpassing 11 percent! This meant that based on the number of times the ad was shown, over 11 percent of the people seeing it were clicking on the button.

Surprisingly, when I asked her if she had seen the results of the campaign, she told me that yes she had and wasn't happy. She explained that the click-through rate of the ad was a dismal 0.1 percent and as a result they would be pulling the campaign down. And they did.

Here I was sitting on perhaps the most effective ad campaign of my career, and I was unable to help the client to see it for what it was because she insisted on measuring something that had nothing to do with the goals of the campaign.

Setting the expectations of your clients is incredibly important. Also, if you're going to measure something, make sure you measure the thing that tells the best story about what you're trying to accomplish. Otherwise, you may be measuring something that not only delivers bad news but is practically worthless.

UNDERSTANDING KEY PERFORMANCE INDICATORS (KPIS)

Successful online ad campaigns are based on accurately measuring the right things—but what are they?

If we said to you "go and measure that group of people over there," how would you approach the task? For starters, it's a really vague instruction. Measure what in particular? You could certainly start by measuring people's height or perhaps weight. You might measure how big their feet are or how long their hands are. You might even record data covering physical characteristics, such as hair color, eye color, skin color, and birthmarks.

The main problem with this directive is that we wouldn't really know what we should measure until we first knew what we planned on doing with the data.

Asking somebody to step on a scale to measure their weight is a simple task. But if all you had was a yardstick, then attempting to use it to measure a person's weight would be a ludicrous idea.

During a digital campaign there are lots of things that can be measured, but unless you know what tools to use and what you plan to do with the data you collect, the task could be pointless.

When we measure campaign results we first need to:

- Understand what tools are available to get the job done
- Understand specifically what to measure
- Understand what story we hope to tell with the data we collect

For example, let's say that a hot dog vendor at a local ballpark wants to measure how many glasses of beer she sells every day. Let's also agree that her inventory system is rather primitive and she's working without a cash register or computer to help her along. The bottom line is that she doesn't have the time or inclination to carefully record every sale but still needs to know how many beers she is selling for reordering and accounting purposes.

The easiest approach is to simply count the beer cups she has on hand at the start of the day and compare that number with the number of beer cups left at the end of the day. The resulting answer will provide the information she needs. In this case, the number of beer cups leaving the stand daily is the KPI. Measuring that one thing will give the vendor the insight she needs.

Key performance indicators don't have to be complex to be effective. The secret of effective marketing measurement and analytics often comes down to defining the question you want an answer to.

For example, let's say that a movie studio is planning on releasing a new movie that promises to be a summer blockbuster. The studio plans to run a number of online campaigns focused on raising awareness about the movie, campaigns that include online branded games, downloads of apps, and placing trailers for the movie on popular sites. While all of these efforts can certainly lead to brand awareness, the one thing that none of these efforts can do is tell the movie studio executives what they most want to know: how many tickets are they going to sell?

Success in the movie business is based on a "butts in seats" scenario. Advertising, unless somehow directly tied in with ticket sales, isn't going to be a good indicator of success in that area. Or is it?

Because the digital realm is fully interactive, it offers options not available in more traditional advertising channels. Everything a consumer does online offers marketers a little bit of feedback. This means that when a consumer goes to a website and plays a game or downloads an icon or some wallpaper or a mobile app, all of those actions can be recorded and measured.

While none of these events can directly indicate whether a consumer will also buy a ticket to see the movie in a theater, a combination of different data sets can indicate a strong probability. These KPIs need to be developed slowly and over time. However, by knowing what came before the purchase decision, marketers can start to gain a better sense of cause and effect.

For example, let's say that the studio decides to create a Facebook page as part of its promotion efforts. On the Facebook page, apart from the movie trailer, the marketers create a forum where visitors can talk about the movie with other visitors, can indicate that they like the movie or the Facebook page, and can even share that link with their Facebook friends. While these individual actions don't directly indicate that the online interactions will result in ticket sales, over time the data will show that a certain percentage of the interactions did lead to sales.

This means that a movie studio that carefully looks at this data in the future will be able to do a better job extrapolating what the box office results will be based upon the social media interactions. What this means for advertisers is that if they are able to accurately measure elements of their online campaigns, they can then use that data to more effectively project what the box office results will be.

In many cases KPIs end up indirectly measuring things that are hard to measure directly.

Again, campaign success is based on knowing before the campaign even runs what you would like the endgame to be. By asking the right questions you will find it's only a matter of looking at different data points to determine which ones can be used to help answer those questions.

SETTING DIGITAL CAMPAIGN BENCHMARKS

Effective digital advertising is not about single campaigns but a process of measurement and optimization over time.

In order to progress we have to know where we've been. For example, if our goal was to be able to run a four-minute mile, then somewhere along the way we have to measure how long it takes us to run a mile. If your first attempt shows that you currently run a mile in approximately 8 ½ minutes, then that information is helpful (and perhaps a bit disheartening) by showing you how your current results match up against your desired ones.

But that initial measurement is a fantastic benchmark. Now you have a time that you hope to beat during your next run. By changing different variables, such as running shoes, exercise routines, nutrition, etc., you have a line in the sand that you can try to beat. Over time you may find that your time to run a mile slips below eight minutes and then seven minutes and then six minutes. As each new time is revealed, it becomes the new benchmark to be used for comparison purposes.

The same thing holds true for your online advertising campaign. If you set out to create a Google AdWords campaign, you'll find it hard to know what to expect from your campaign results if you've never run a campaign before. The first time out you're going to try to do your best and use the results from that campaign as a benchmark to compare future campaigns against. This means that if the results do not meet your expectations, you can start to figure out what new tweaks and changes to the existing campaign you might put into play so that the future results will beat the current ones. In this way we are able to optimize the campaign because we already have an understanding of where we've been and where we would eventually like to be.

Overall, setting benchmarks helps focus the targeting of your marketing. Over time that target will be redefined, and as the benchmarks change even the parameters of the campaign will evolve. But by setting an initial benchmark, campaign managers have a goal to shoot for and surpass during their next campaign.

IT'S ALL ABOUT CONVERSION

Measuring click-through rates is perfect if all you want to measure is the number of people who click on an ad. But who wants that?

We're not big fans of the click-through rate metric mostly because it tells marketers very little about what their campaigns are accomplishing. That's not to say that it can't be a useful metric if you want a better sense of traffic flow, but it is often a highly abused metric that marketers use hoping it is synonymous with campaign success. It isn't.

Measuring points of meaningful consumer contact and conversion is the only thing that matters. Conversion goals are specific things that take place as a result of consumer interactions. While click-through can certainly assist in helping consumers get to a point of conversion, that click is rarely the point of conversion.

So what is conversion? Well, it's really anything that an advertiser wants to measure to help determine whether the campaign reached its primary objectives or not. For example, conversion can be based on something as simple as collecting e-mail addresses. If a campaign is structured to create a path so that consumers click on a web ad or search link and then go to a landing page where they can sign up for a free webinar by leaving their name and e-mail address, then being able to measure the number of new e-mail addresses collected is the primary point of conversion. Measuring the number of times the ad was clicked on doesn't tell the right story at all even though the click-through is part of the process.

Measuring conversion means measuring your endgame—what you are really trying to accomplish and why you are spending your money/time/resources.

Let's say that you're responsible for getting a digital display campaign in front of a target audience. Let's also say that the goal of the campaign is not merely to drive traffic to a landing page but to encourage consumers to download a free app from that landing page.

You buy media on six different sites you believe will allow you to get the right message in front of the right people. At the end of the first 30 days you compare the CTR results of each of the sites.

Because you have limited resources and you want to make sure that your money is being spent wisely, and so you are most likely going to do a reassessment on which sites are giving you love and which are not. In the chart in figure 2.1 we can easily see that the click-through results for sites A, D, and F are easily beating those of sites B, C, and E.

We can also easily see that site B is the weakest CTR player, getting only a 0.2 percent rate. Financial logic dictates that we dump that site and either put that money toward site A, D, or F or find a new site altogether. The bottom line is that site B is a dog that needs to be put out of its misery.

Or is it?

If you only measure click-through rate, then it appears that site B isn't pulling its weight. But does measuring CTR tell us the right story? What happens if we measure the overall conversion percentages for each of the sites instead?

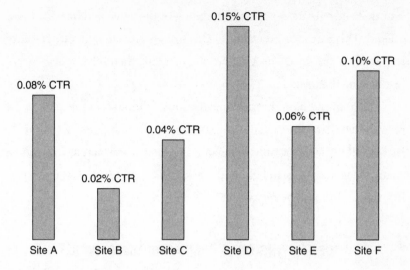

Figure 2.1   Site click-through rate comparisons

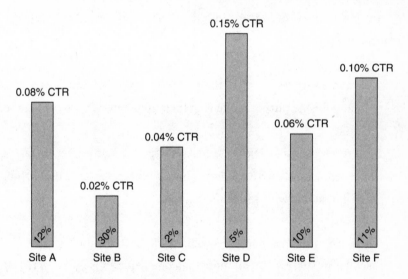

Figure 2.2   Six site click-through rate comparisons—CTR vs. conversion

The conversion information for this campaign tells a very different story about the effectiveness of the campaign. With the conversion data in place (see figure 2.2). We can see that site B is actually a bit of a gem. In fact, compared to site D, site B is almost on a par from a conversion standpoint.

By the way, it's not uncommon for a well-targeted site to do a better job getting higher conversion rates because the people most likely to visit that site have a deeper understanding of the value and benefits being offered. This can mean that low click-through rates may be the result of respondents already doing a better job qualifying themselves; they are not just kicking the tires.

The bottom line is that making decisions without looking at all of the relevant data can be costly. In the first scenario, the advertiser was ready to jettison site B without fully understanding that it was actually the goose laying the golden eggs. In light of the new data, it is site C that is underperforming and should be reevaluated.

IDENTIFYING CORE CAMPAIGN OBJECTIVES

Brand awareness and direct response campaigns are based on two very different digital advertising objectives.

In most areas of advertising there are two primary campaign objectives:

1. Brand awareness—where the goal is to introduce consumers to a brand for the purpose of having them remember that brand in the future.
2. Direct response—where the goal is to persuade consumers to take a specific action, such as calling a phone number, visiting a dealership, or interacting with something online.

These are not interchangeable objectives. Each requires a different approach for its success. Yet, on more than one request for proposal (RFP) during our careers we have seen advertisers try to position their campaign as being focused on branding and direct response at the same time.

With this type of thinking the challenge is how consumers are expected to react to each type of campaign objective. For example, with a branding awareness campaign the goal is to help consumers become more familiar with the brand. This is often done by using more traditional marketing approaches, such as reach and frequency, in which the greatest number of consumers are shown an ad frequently. At the end of the campaign it is hoped that those consumers will now have a greater familiarity with a brand that was previously unfamiliar to them.

With this understanding let's say that we create an online display ad campaign. If a consumer sees this ad for the first time, we can assume that a little bit of the branding message is conveyed. However, to be more effective the advertiser will want to reach that consumer again to reinforce that branding message. This means that if the consumer is shown an ad over and over, subsequent viewings will help to raise overall brand awareness (up to a certain point).

Now let's consider the goal of a direct response campaign. A direct response campaign is designed to encourage consumers to take some sort of action. If we were to run a similar digital display ad campaign promoting some type of direct response, then a consumer seeing the ad for the first time may not find the message personally relevant and may not take any action. This also means that if consumers are shown the ad again, it probably isn't going to make the process any more relevant. In fact, if the ad were shown repeatedly, it might start to irritate consumers enough to lead to negative branding. So, on the one hand we have a model in which repeating a message can lead to greater and greater success, and on the other hand we have a model in which repeating the message is going to be less and less useful.

The reality is that branding and direct response are two different goals. Once again, understanding the ultimate goal of the campaign before getting started is incredibly important and if poorly planned can end up negatively affecting the overall campaign results.

IF YOU FAIL TO PLAN, THEN PLAN TO FAIL

Setting clear campaign goals is paramount to any advertising campaign. It's also necessary to adjust those goals continuously.

Every campaign will be different. The channel being used, the audience being targeted, and even the message being conveyed will all combine to create new scenarios and new challenges. But without a goal you have nothing to aim for. When you have nothing to aim for, you have nothing to measure against. If you have nothing to measure against, then you have no way of determining whether you're heading in the right direction.

The bottom line is that marketers use best practices when planning and executing their campaigns but are also willing to make adjustments along the way in order to do a better job of achieving the desired results. The alternative is to pretend that you are doing everything perfectly the first time. Since this is rarely true, you're just setting yourself up for a big hurt.

So, what goals should you be setting for your campaigns? Obviously, this depends on what you're trying to accomplish, but here's a list of objectives that can effectively be used to measure campaign effectiveness regardless of whether you use e-mail, social media, display ads, or anything else to reach consumers:

- Total sales
- Campaign ROI
- Campaign conversion rate
- Cost per lead
- Cost per sale
- Top producing ads, landing pages, e-mails, etc.
- Revenue per click

The bottom line is that you need to know what metrics mesh with your business goals. You're not in the business of advertising, you're in the business of making money. Measure the right things, and you will stay in that business.

ASKING THE RIGHT QUESTIONS TO GET THE RIGHT ANSWERS

Campaign success isn't based on collecting data. It's based on collecting the right data to tell the right story.

Imagine that a store has just opened up on Main Street. With a fair amount of hoopla, the owners drape their grand opening banners in front of the store, run some ads in the local newspaper, stick some flyers under windshield wipers, and do whatever else they can to let people in the area know that they're open for business. After all, they reason, all of this advertising is being done to drive traffic through the front door of the store.

The various ad channels do the trick, and prospects start to show up. The store owner has carefully created a way of counting the number of people who enter the store by putting a light beam counter on the front door. After the first week the owner is delighted to see that over 3,000 people have entered the store. It appears that the campaigns are incredibly successful!

Or are they?

The problem with this kind of scenario is that like click-through rates, the counter fails to measure the impact each visitor has on helping the business owners reach their financial goals. For example, if 3,000 people visit the store in the first week but nobody buys anything, is that better or worse than a similar store that only has one visitor per week but that visitor makes a purchase?

As you might guess, success in advertising and business isn't only about driving traffic. It's about driving traffic that results in some type of conversion. In most cases conversion is tied directly to financial goals for a specific action taken on the part of a consumer.

So let's back up for a moment: what are advertisers running an advertising campaign trying to accomplish? Certainly having ads that attract consumers' attention and encourage them to become engaged is part of the process. But ultimately the number of people who click on an ad is less important than the number of people who click on an ad and then go on to do something the advertiser really wanted them to do. Think about it—most web ads are nothing more than large buttons designed to try to engage consumers so that they will click on them to learn more. Realistically, there's not much room in the standard ad banner to tell much of a story. As a result, it's generally more of a come-on placed there in the hope that consumers will click so that they can drill a little deeper to learn more about the value and benefits being offered.

At least that's the plan.

However, the current reality is that the average number of times that consumers click on an ad is about 0.3 to 0.5 out of every 1,000 times it is shown. Yeah, it's not really an impressive number. Now, if you stay with this average and buy ad impressions in chunks of 1,000 units (also known as a CPM or cost per thousand) that it's going to take quite a few impressions to create any real interest among consumers.

By the way, here's the formula for measuring click-through rate: number of clicks / number of impressions $\times$ 100 = CTR. In our scenario it would look like 750 $\div$ 250,000 $\times$ 100 = 0.3%.

Is this good? Well, let's do some basic mathematics: if an advertiser sets out to buy 250,000 ad impressions and can expect somewhere around 750 clicks as part of the campaign, is the campaign successful?

Well, the answer depends on how much it cost to buy those impressions and on what takes place after a consumer clicks on the ad. From a pricing standpoint, let's just say that the CPM is $4. This means that if 250 CPM "units" are purchased, then the cost of the media buy is $1,000. In this case, it means that each click that the advertiser received cost $1.25 to acquire. Again, is this good or bad? Well, we're not there yet because we have no way of knowing if there was a return on investment because measuring the click-through rate alone doesn't tell us the entire story. It also doesn't tell us what happened after the click.

Advertising best practices are about driving consumers to a point of conversion. This conversion can take many different forms including acquiring data, getting a consumer to take a specific action, such as downloading a PDF, or making a sale. What an advertiser wants to measure from a commercial standpoint depends on the campaign goals that have been set.

Let's say in our scenario the goal is to sell a product. After consumers click on the web banner, they are taken to a landing page that tells a deeper story about the offer and encourages those consumers to become customers by making a purchase. The reality of this type of model is that not all people who click on the ad are also going to become buyers. In fact, we can pretty much guarantee that only a small percentage of people who click on the ad are going to convert in any way. Again, for the sake of our scenario, let's say that 10 percent of the people who click on the ad went on to purchase the item being offered. In this case, it means that 75 people ended up converting. So, does this mean the campaign is a success?

We're not there yet! Without knowing the value of each conversion, we can't start to figure out whether the campaign even paid for itself. But let's say that each sale that is made means $15 for the advertiser. With this information we can do a quick calculation and look at the number of conversions, in this case 75, then at how much money those conversions brought in, and when multiplied by $15 for each, this brings us to a grand total of $1,125. Since the media buy costs $1,000, that leaves a profit of $125 for the advertiser. Not a huge profit, but a profit nonetheless.

The main takeaway is that when you have a clear campaign goal you can measure against that goal. The feedback received from measuring a campaign can be used to reevaluate goals to make sure they are realistic and also serve as a benchmark that can be used as a point of comparison in the future. However, if you never measure your progress because of a fear of failure then you will never be able to determine your success either.

CHAPTER 3

DEFINING ONLINE AUDIENCES

If the secret to effective online advertising is reaching the right people with the right message, how do we find the right people?

Imagine you are attending a baseball game in a stadium. Around you are thousands and thousands of other people. As you scan the crowd, you see men and women, some old and some very young. You see people of different ethnic heritages, socioeconomic backgrounds, and political leanings. Some of them are rooting for your team, and some are rooting for the other team. Some are watching the game with a deep intensity while others are talking with friends and not paying much attention to the game.

Despite these differences, at this moment all these people have one thing in common: they are all experiencing a baseball game at the same time and in the same place.

Let's say that you were tasked with dividing all the people in the stadium into smaller targeted audience segments. What criteria would you use to group people together in a meaningful way? Would you approach the challenge using traditional demographics like gender, age, earnings potential, and place of residence? Or would you use more of a psychographic targeting approach and divide them based on their beliefs, attitudes, and opinions or perhaps religious preferences, political preferences, hobbies, and lifestyles?

The obvious answer these questions is that it would depend entirely on what you were trying to accomplish in the long run. The criteria you would use would depend greatly on who you most wanted to have a conversation with.

As marketers, we need to know more about what makes the people whom we consider our customers behave the way they do. We need to understand what they want and need in their lives. We need to understand what problems they're trying to solve and how the solutions we provide can help them. We need to have a deeper understanding of the things that make them happy and unhappy before we can ever effectively identify who they are and how we can help them.

We talk a lot in this book about the idea of reaching people. In the digital realm the goal is never to reach everybody. Instead, we need to identify and parse out all of the different parts that make the perfect customer for our products and services. We need to know what these people are thinking about, what is missing from their lives, what inspires them, what they will respond to, and what they most identify with. We need to have a realistic picture of how our products and services make people's lives better and how we can cultivate meaningful relationships with these people so that when they're ready to buy, they buy from us.

This is not an easy task. But there are a few things that we can do to make the process more approachable. The first is to identify just what it means to be a person.

THE HUMAN EXPERIENCE

What does it mean to be human? The answer to this question is often the key to creating effective online advertising campaigns.

We could try to answer this question from a number of different angles. Let's say you work in the field of robotics and you're trying to create an artificial intelligence that simulates human thought and reasoning. In this case you're probably going to focus on decision-making processes and how people learn and understand. As you might imagine the outcome of this exploration can be very complex.

We might also look at this question through the eyes of an anthropologist. How does society affect the behavior of a population? How do core beliefs and social norms drive people's behaviors? What characteristics are unique to any culture or population, and what does that mean?

As marketers we are continuously pursuing similar paths of exploration. To be an effective marketer means understanding human needs and motivations and how they can be addressed and met. Marketers need to understand what motivates people to take action. They need to understand how human beings decide not only what it is that they want but how they intend to get it. We also need to understand what people won't do.

While we have very little argument that human beings are complex creatures, the core of who we are and how we make decisions is actually very basic. In fact, most human beings spend the majority of their time focused on meeting their biological need to maintain a biological balance. This need for homeostasis is a driving force behind many of the social, emotional, and biological needs we experience.

In 1943, American psychologist and behaviorist Abraham Maslow published a paper entitled "A Theory of Human Motivation" (published in *Psychology Review* 50 (4), 370–96; the article is now in the public domain). In this paper he explored what has come to be known as Maslow's hierarchy of needs, which is a model that outlines the different fundamental needs of people (physiological, safety, belongingness and love, esteem, and self-actualization and self-transcendence) and how each of these needs affects individual behaviors and motivates people to take action.

Generally laid out as a pyramid (see figure 3.1), Maslow's model looks at the different stages of a person's physical and emotional well-being. Each stage represents an area of human needs and their fulfillment. For example, the first layer covers physiological needs. These include the motivations and tasks we undertake to keep ourselves alive and healthy, such as the ongoing need to breathe, eat, drink, have sex, sleep, and remove toxins from the body.

The second layer of the pyramid, which explores safety issues such as personal safety, employment security, morality, love of family, maintaining personal health, and protection of property is generally not even on

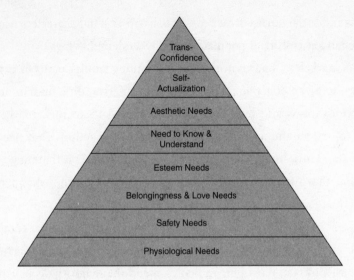

Figure 3.1   Maslow's hierarchy of needs

our radar if our most basic needs aren't being met. In short, people who haven't had anything to eat for three days aren't going to care about getting their car cleaned and waxed or their resume polished up so that it will land them their dream job. In fact, until physiological needs are met, few people can think about little else. Nature has wired us so that these needs are nearly impossible to ignore.

Fortunately, most of the people we come into contact with are healthy and their fundamental needs are being met. As marketers, our jobs are easier then because we can more easily address ongoing needs that aren't tied directly into survival and health and can instead address consumers' lifestyle needs.

This brings us to our main point regarding human behavior: while we readily acknowledge that human needs and behaviors can be complex, the majority of human behavior often comes down to two simple states. Human beings continuously change their behaviors in order to:

1. Avoid pain/loss
2. Maximize pleasure/gain

Think about your own behavior for a moment. How do you make decisions? Often decisions are automatic and based on our biology. For example, we don't have to spend a lot of time weighing the pros and cons of removing our hand from a hot stove. We don't have to consciously remember to breathe or keep our heart beating or salivate. Likewise, a desperate need for sleep will eventually take care of itself whether or not we consciously make the decision to go to bed.

Yet, we also live in a world in which we make hundreds of decision every day about maintaining comfort in our bodies and environments. These range from making plans for our next meal to where we want to spend our next vacation to the types of relationships we want to develop. We weigh things using a combination of rational (at least to us) and motivational thoughts. In most cases these decisions are simple and can be combined with other simple decisions to help us make bigger and more complex decisions.

Because of what we already understand about the human decision-making process, we can often predict what an individual will do in certain circumstances. For example, new parents may have little idea of what the day-to-day process of rearing children really holds for them, but veteran parents can predict with ease just what type of decisions new parents will be making, from figuring out the minivan features that will best fit their needs to figuring out the best schools to consider.

In many other day-to-day situations people rely on their previous experiences and personal understanding of the world as a foundation for their behavior and decision making.

Let's say that you have decided to go out a restaurant for dinner. What criteria do you use to select a meal? You may avoid the eggplant parmesan because you already know that you don't care for eggplant. You may choose the spaghetti and meatballs instead of the ravioli because the last time you visited this restaurant you had the ravioli, and while it was good, trying something new adds a little diversity to life and that too makes you happy.

Ordering a meal in a restaurant is hardly an earth-shattering decision process. But every other decision we make follows a similar path. Let's look at a more complex example.

Let's say that your desire is to become wealthy. Through your understanding of the world you know that the majority of people make money by working at a job. You understand that making money is the foundation of becoming wealthy. However, you also know from past experience that working at a job is sometimes boring or hard and not a lot of fun. So on the one hand you have a desire to maximize your pleasure by acquiring wealth, and on the other hand you're trying to avoid the pain that often comes with working hard.

You might also consider making an investment in higher education so that you can earn a degree that will allow you to make even more money in a job. Once again, while the education may present an economic point of discomfort (tuition costs and having to study), that pain can be offset by the understanding that your hard work will eventually contribute to greater pleasure in the form of a satisfying career and more money through your employment.

Are there ways to get money other than having a day job? Absolutely. One way is to rob a bank. After all, banks have lots of money, and if money is what you're trying to acquire, then robbing a bank can certainly meet that goal. However, the more socially savvy among us also understand that not only is robbing a bank morally and ethically wrong and highly illegal, but the downside for attempting to rob a bank can be loss of freedom or even loss of life. When you weigh the pros against the cons, or in this case the gain against the loss, robbing a bank doesn't really seem worth it. In the long run you're much better off getting an annoying day job and using that as your springboard toward wealth.

Fortunately, for most of us the decisions we make day-to-day aren't life-or-death decisions. But our motivations as individuals still come down to a few fundamentals based upon our desire for gain and our avoidance of pain.

UNDERSTANDING HUMAN MOTIVATION

Our job is not to wave products in front of a consumer's face but to give people a reason to want to pay attention.

Let's deconstruct human motivation for a moment. What motivates people to do anything? Often motivation depends on the experiences and circumstances of the individual. Nevertheless, over the years we have defined a number of biological, social, and emotional motivators that drive behavior and are often used by marketers to create points of persuasion.

- **We Are Always Striving to Maintain Balance**—Biological homeostasis is a huge driving force in our lives. Homeostasis is the balanced relationship between our brains and bodies, and it is responsible for keeping us alive and comfortable by allowing us to feel pain so that we can minimize or eliminate it. For example, hunger is our stomach's way to tell the brain that we need to put more fuel into our bodies. If we ignore signs of hunger, those pangs will get stronger and stronger until we do something to make them go away. The same thing holds true for managing thirst as well as for our need for sleep. The pain of hunger, thirst, and tiredness and even sexual desire will persist until we do something to make the pain go away.

- **We Desire Certainty**—Part of the human survival instinct is to strive to maintain a balance between our expectations and our reality. We want to know that when we go to bed at night, the world will pretty much be the same place in the morning. We want to expect that when we park our car at night, it will still be there in the morning. We want to believe that the job that we maintain so we can make money will continue to be there for us. Of course, things can change abruptly regardless of our certainty. A house fire can dramatically change our lives, as can a stolen car or the loss of a job. Therefore, we often concern ourselves (sometimes unnecessarily) and worry about the loss of certainty and make decisions to do things that will reinforce that certainty.

- **We Desire Uncertainty**—While it may seem paradoxical based on the previous point, one main problem with certainty is that it's boring. While on the one hand we desire continuity in our lives, a life that is never changing also makes for a rather dull existence.

We like variety in our lives as long as it doesn't upset other things that we find most important. Having "adventures," whether on vacation or at home, allows us to step outside of our normal circumstances and experience something new. We also challenge certainty by putting ourselves in uncertain circumstances, such as on amusement park rides. We know deep down that going on a roller coaster isn't going to result in our deaths (probably!), but we also like to fool our brains into thinking that we're walking on the edge. The resulting fear and excitement is a welcome state change over that of sheer boredom and sameness.

Likewise, watching movies and television allows us to experience state change as we shift our perspective by living vicariously through others. While we understand intellectually that these experiences aren't real, it's hard to argue that point when you can feel yourself tearing up while watching a sad movie or experiencing a jolt of adrenaline during an action film.

- **We Want To Feel Significant**—Human beings need to feel significant. We need to feel that we have purpose and that our lives have meaning. Very few people are willing to believe that their lives are meaningless and have no purpose. That's pretty close to being emotionally dead. We want to matter even if it's just to one other person. For some people creating meaningful relationships with other people allows them to feel good about themselves because it increases their social significance and allows them to be a part of something larger than themselves. For others, significance is about helping other people or creating a legacy that will live on after their death.

- **We Want Be Connected to Others and to Be Loved**—The old hermit who lives in the shack on the edge of town is a model of social dysfunction. Human beings are hardwired to be social and to be connected to other people. This drive propels us to do things to sustain and improve our social connectivity. We will often do things (sometimes incredibly stupid things!) to express our desire to love and be loved by others.

- **We Want To Make Progress**—A static life is a boring life. We want to evolve, and we want to change as we grow. We want the sense that we are heading toward something meaningful and not just standing in one place. This motivation causes us to take on difficult and even uncomfortable tasks because we have the ability to look forward in time and understand that our efforts can lead us toward a desired conclusion.

Again, marketing is not just about putting messages in front of consumers but is based on communicating ways that increase individuals' pleasure or reduce pain.

PURSUING PLEASURE

When we talk about feeling good, there are a variety of different factors that most people associate with personal pleasure. Personal pleasure includes experiencing:

- A feeling of success
- A sense of freedom
- A sense of comfort
- A sense of security
- A sense of adventure
- Falling in love

Conversely, there are a variety of negative values that most people will actively avoid as pain points. These include:

- Feeling frustrated
- Feeling anger
- Experiencing physical pain
- Feeling fear
- Experiencing social humiliation
- Feeling depressed

While both positive and negative emotions are universal in defining what motivates people, how we define the significance of the pleasure/pain relationship can differ greatly from one individual to another. In short, our experience and beliefs about the world are going to deeply mold our relationship with each emotion, whether positive or negative.

For example, desiring security and desiring adventure are both positive values. However, an individual who craves a sense of security and considers that to be the utmost of personal pleasure is probably going to be at odds with people whose love of adventure is the highest priority in their lives. While both can be considered motivators on the pleasure side of things, it's probably a safe bet that people who treasure security above all else are going to have a very different set of expectations for their lives than those who look upon a life of adventure and daring as being the be-all and end-all—especially when it comes to jumping out of a perfectly good airplane with a parachute.

The same holds true on the negative side of the equation. While each of these behavioral factors may be a negative motivator, once again it's up to the individual to determine which one is most personally significant. For example, some people may avoid doing something primarily out of fear of physical pain while others will willingly experience the pain if it means that they don't have to suffer any social humiliation. As you can imagine, when you start to cross-reference each of these positive and negative behavioral emotions in the preceding list with one another, you can create some very complex models.

However, our purpose in this book isn't to run through all the idiosyncrasies of human behavior but to make it clear that as marketers (and communicators) we need to understand the fundamentals of the human psyche in order to do a better job of creating messages that resonate with the people we're trying to reach. We also need to reach the right people with those messages.

Effective marketing is based upon getting consumers to behave in a way that corresponds to the marketer's campaign goals, such as making a purchase. While it may seem like a simple enough process to say "I have something for sale, please buy it," people make buying decisions based on how taking a specific action will affect them emotionally. Consumers buy for personal reasons. They buy because there is a clear and personal benefit to them. They buy because it makes them feel good to do so.

As marketers, one of the biggest challenges we face is recognizing that our customers are not all alike. Each has a unique perspective on the world and is truly an individual. And while these different people may share common characteristics, it's still very difficult to get good results from campaigns that focus on a few shared characteristics, such as gender, age. and zip code.

So how do we identify and define these unique and personal characteristics? That's a good question.

SELLING THROUGH SELF-PERCEPTION

What makes us uniquely us? It's a hard question to answer even though we know ourselves better than anybody else does.

One of the primary challenges we face as marketers is being able to define the needs, interests, attitudes, opinions, beliefs, and other perceptions of the people we are trying to reach. The main challenge doesn't stem from how we perceive these prospects and customers but from how they perceive themselves. One of the primary disconnects in most marketing campaigns of the past fifty years or more has been the idea that people can be easily defined based upon demographic data.

While we agree that demographics have a place in marketing, knowing a consumer's age, salary range, gender, ZIP code, and marital status rarely tells a meaningful story about how that person lives and what motivates them to make choices.

Demographics offer marketers data. Even if it's accurate data, is it meaningful data? The answer to this, as with most questions in marketing, is that it depends!

Early audience targeting was basically a case of marketers "fishing where the fish are." By using data, such as ZIP codes, marketers could determine areas where more affluent people lived. Does this mean that everybody who lives in a particular ZIP code area is affluent? No. Does it mean that everybody who lives in that particular ZIP code area is going to be interested in the same offer? Probably not. But the ZIP code data did give marketers a place from which to cast their lines even if they weren't going to catch all of the fish.

However, the main problem with this model is that it's based on vague generalizations. To assume that people living in an affluent ZIP code area are going to be more willing to buy a product is often incorrect. To assume that a sporting magazine that focuses on football coverage is only going to be interesting to men is incorrect. To assume that a new album released by a young band is only going to be of interest to people under the age of 25 is often also incorrect.

This isn't to say that marketers cannot safely assume that people who live in more affluent areas have more money or that more men than women are football fans or that more people under the age of 25 are fans of new music. But this type of thinking also ends up getting in the way of finding more accurate ways to reach affluent consumers who *have an interest* in an offer. Of course, there are plenty of passionate female football fans (and plenty of men who couldn't care less), and there are plenty of people in their fifties who absolutely love hearing about new bands (and have more spending power than younger audiences).

Instead of making generalizations about likes, desires, and intentions using overly simple data points, such as age and gender, doesn't it make more sense to better understand the makeup of a hugely passionate football fan regardless of gender or anything else? Doesn't it make sense to market new music to *all people who* show they are active buyers of new releases regardless of their age? Absolutely.

The digital marketing realm gives advertisers and marketers the opportunity to stop guessing about what their prospects and customers want and instead learn how to meet those needs by asking the right questions and then looking for the right data. Online we can now get a more complete picture of individual consumers by asking the right questions about that consumer's needs, interests, and intentions.

Using psychographic targeting methods allows us to get a better understanding of the needs and interests of individual consumers who visit web pages, click on ads, leave comments in social media channels, and generally interact in the dynamic environment that is the web.

Psychographics is a study of personality, values, attitudes, interests, and lifestyles. It is sometimes referred to as IAO targeting (standing for interests, attitudes, and opinions). While psychographics offers a much deeper and richer way to analyze human behavior, it's also more complicated because unlike more traditional demographic targeting, the variables used to identify individual personality traits are all over the map. But the good news is that because every consumer is unique, looking for characteristics that help to define an individual person's needs and interests brings us a lot closer to making a meaningful direct connection with that person.

SOWING AND REAPING AUDIENCE DATA

How easily can you define and determine the characteristics that make up a target audience? It's often easier than you think.

Let's say you're hanging out in a park one spring day. All around you people are engaged in outdoor activities. As you sit on the bench, you start to play a little game with yourself: can I identify targeting characteristics about these people by just watching them?

You discover quickly that you are readily able to identify people by their gender, age range, and maybe even socioeconomic factors. You might be able to even gauge marital status by looking for people with probable spouses or with children or people who are wearing engagement or wedding rings.

You're probably going to do a fairly good job of accurately identifying these data points just by watching people. But here's a hard question to answer: is this observed data "meaningful"?

It's generally not hard to create a list of characteristics about a person, but it's very challenging to identify characteristics that mesh with how that person sees himself or herself. These characteristics are the meaningful data points, and they rarely emerge just from observation. But online consumers offer us a much richer view of who they are and what they find important and personally relevant.

In the online world, just by watching, marketers can do a better job of gathering data that tells a better story. For example, if your job was to sell pet food, then it stands to reason that you would be very interested in communicating with pet owners who buy food for their pets. But unless you are able to observe a person out walking a dog (and cats usually don't appreciate being taken for walks!), then it's generally hard to discern whether someone you see walking by owns a pet.

However, the web offers some unique opportunities to observe people. For starters, a great number of publisher sites provide very targeted information. A website that caters to veterinarian needs, animal health, and other information generally of interest to pet owners is going to offer a prime targeting opportunity for an advertiser. You don't have to know anything else about the people who visit this website other than that they probably own pets. This contextual targeting approach is certainly not new. Advertisers have been using magazines and other specialty publications to reach target audiences like this for years. But what is new is that marketers can start to look for other behaviors or cues that indicate a specific consumer's areas of interest and so can to some extent predict future behaviors.

MINING BEHAVIORAL DATA

Data is like gasoline. If it sits in a container untouched, it is practically useless. It needs to be used to create meaning.

Let's head back to the park for a moment. Instead of creating a list of identifying characteristics for everybody who walks by, let's start looking for specific cues and indicators of behavior that help us to better define a specific type of consumer.

For starters, you might notice that there are lots of people who are out for a run in the park. While not all of them might consider themselves to be avid runners, by observing how they dress, the brands of running shoes they wear, the athletic clothing they wear, the musical player they are listening to, the sunglasses they are wearing, and other very basic considerations of attire and equipment, you can start to develop a pretty interesting list of different ways marketers may start a meaningful conversation with individual consumers.

That's not to say that every runner in the park is going to want to buy new clothing and equipment, but the fact that these people currently own attire related to running is an indicator of how seriously they take their sport. Chances are also good that they may need to upgrade their attire or equipment in the future.

What about the people riding bicycles? Are they riding alone or with friends? Are they wearing helmets and other safety gear? What kind of condition are their bicycles in? Are they riding high-end and potentially expensive racing bikes or are they using obvious rentals?

And what about the people having a picnic underneath the large oak tree? What are their stories? What do we know about the dog walkers? And the college kids playing Frisbee?

The diversity of the people in a park might be enough to give us pause. After all, just making some simple observations can yield a lot of data. But the good news is that most marketers aren't trying to reach everybody. This means that it's a lot easier to focus on just identifying those characteristics that match with a specific marketing and targeting need. After all, we only want to reach the right people.

However, before we can do a sufficient job of identifying our perfect audience, we first need to have a better understanding of the relationship between our products and services and consumers' individual needs.

Practical Wisdom—Let's say you're visiting your local mall one day and you're approached by a person who asks you if you would like to participate in an experiment. In this experiment the researcher offers you one of two choices for a snack. One is an ice cream sundae and the other is a bowl of brussels sprouts. You are told that the focus of this experiment is to get a better sense of which snack the average person prefers.

We feel pretty confident that without doing actual research here, we could accurately predict the outcome of this particular experiment! It seems obvious that the average person is going to choose the ice cream sundae over the brussels sprouts because they will prefer the pleasure of the sweet dessert over that of the not so sweet vegetable. However, we also feel confident that the choice of the ice cream sundae is not going to be a universal decision. Some individuals participating in this experiment may see positive opportunities for each choice. They may also see a negative side to both.

For example, some people may reason that while the ice cream sundae is a sweet and pleasure-inducing dessert choice, it is also fattening and a poor diet choice for someone looking to lose weight. Eating it could result in emotional pain and regret. Other people may consider both choices and choose the sprouts as a much healthier dietary alternative. This choice in turn may help them to not only benefit from the healthier food but also to feel good about their decision to make a choice that will make them healthier and perhaps live longer. Still other people may automatically choose the brussels sprouts because they are lactose intolerant, and ice cream is already associated with pain in their minds.

Overall, consumers' final decision will be based on their individual life experiences and knowledge of the world.

Let's say that you run a small landscaping company. While you might consider yourself to be in the business of doing backyard makeovers, planting trees, pulling up weeds, and generally beautifying people's property, if you had to explain to somebody else just who your perfect customers are, would you be able to easily answer the question?

Yours might be a company that does the majority of your business in a summer resort area. This may mean that the people you work with mostly are not full-time residents but are people who own vacation homes and may be more affluent than the average resident. This understanding may allow you to offer services that focus on cleaning and sprucing up properties in the spring so that when the owners arrive in the summer, everything is ready to go.

Or you may run a company that works very closely with real estate professionals to help them stage the homes they are trying to sell. By bringing in movable plants and flowers, your company specializes in creating stunning but temporary arrangements that help to inspire homebuyers to make an offer.

Or you could work with homebuilders and other companies specializing in the building trades. After the house is built, it's your job to create beautiful landscapes that match the expectations of the builders and the homeowners.

Once again there's no one-size-fits-all answer. Different landscaping companies are going to offer different services and a different value. This also means that one company may be looking for the perfect customer in one place while another company is going to be looking at a completely different target audience.

So far we've talked about the types of data that marketers can collect by observing online consumers. While much of that data can be valuable and a strong indicator of a possible future behavior, it is mostly still an educated guess. Sometimes the easiest way to get the data we want about consumers is to ask them for it directly. This approach also takes out the guesswork.

Declared data is just what the term says; it's data consumers willingly share in exchange for something they perceive to be of value to them. A very common example of this is the process of collecting e-mail addresses so that the marketer can reach out to a prospect in the future.

As we will discuss in chapter 6 (E-mail Marketing) this approach not only yields valuable data but also sets up a precedent and permission-based marketing path for an advertiser. Many marketers use questionnaires, polls, sweepstakes, and other ways to encourage consumers to provide them with accurate data they can then use to do a better job of aligning their marketing efforts with consumers' needs and interests.

Declared data can range from basic information, such as name and e-mail address to mailing address and phone numbers and other information regarding lifestyle, demographic markers, and other personally relevant data points.

In the digital online universe, who we have our conversations with is paramount to our success as marketers. But as we will explore next, identifying who we need to talk to is only the beginning. It's what we end up saying to them that is going to make the biggest difference in whether our campaigns are successful or not.

CHAPTER 4

CREATING THE PERFECT ONLINE MARKETING MESSAGE

As marketers our job is to communicate with people. This means moving information from the advertising space and into their minds.

We define the message as the understanding, knowledge, or information that is retained by consumers after they are exposed to or interact with an ad.

In most cases a marketing message is a very simple point of communication. Sometimes it is part of an ongoing conversation. Other times it simply plays on a consumer's emotional needs. It can range from being something that boils down to "remember our brand" to something that tells a more complex story. What's most important is that this exchange of information is part of the process that helps shift consumers' perception from where it currently is to where the advertiser wants it to be. Whatever this message is, it needs to be carefully defined so that it meets both the needs of the consumers it is meant for and also meets the advertiser's marketing objectives.

Advertising is about persuasion. Through advertising we try to change people's behaviors and make them do things that will benefit them as well as the advertiser. Advertising is basically a specialized form of communication, and as in all communication, effectiveness depends on an exchange of information.

The message has to navigate through an incredibly harsh environment to be effective and must do the following:

- Compete with literally thousands of other things vying for a consumer's attention during an average day
- Have a very short window of opportunity during which the message is viable and can be delivered
- Understand that no single message will be meaningful or relevant for all members of a target audience
- Understand that most consumers are not open or receptive to receiving marketing messages
- Understand that most people don't consciously pay attention to the vast majority of messages they do receive

For these reasons it's important that each message is created to deliver a specific understanding to a specific target audience. This means that to be effective the message must address consumers' deepest needs and desires.

Several years ago we created a message creation matrix to help us better define the core of the marketing messages we wanted our campaigns to deliver. Not surprisingly, the foundation of this process depends on who you are talking to and what they most want to hear and need to understand.

Each audience and audience segment is unique. This means that marketing messages need to be unique as well and address specific emotional and market needs. The common use of a "one-size-fits-all" marketing message is not only hugely inefficient but represents a wasted opportunity for marketers to address specific consumer needs and interests. Not all consumers are the same, and they buy products and services for different and personal reasons. By identifying those differences, savvy marketers can do a better job of creating better targeted ads that address those specific needs.

EXPLORING COMMUNICATIONS MODELS

Living in interactive space is nothing new. Human communication that doesn't rely on interactivity is the exception and not the rule.

When we look at a basic interpersonal communication model, we start by defining the roles of the people who are communicating. Because the goal of all communication is to effectively move a message from one point to another, it also means that the people sharing that message must be able to create their side of the conversation but also understand and process information from other people.

In the model in figure 4.1, each of the individuals in an interpersonal communication model takes on the role of information sender and receiver. When the individuals are able to create and send messages as needed as well as receive messages, a conversation can be sustained.

However, the main challenge with all forms of communication is that there is always a layer of noise between any individuals having a conversation. Noise is best defined as anything that can get in the way of the message being successfully transmitted or received. For example, noise could quite literally be represented by noise. Two people trying to have a conversation are going to find it difficult if they're dealing with the sound of a loud truck going by or an airplane flying overhead.

But noise can be represented by anything else that can slow or stop the flow of communication. For example, two people who speak completely different languages are going to have difficulty communicating even if they can hear each other clearly. This would also be classified as noise.

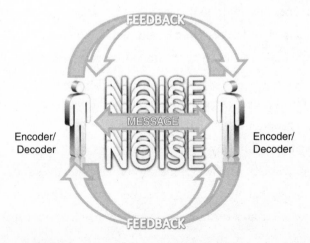

Figure 4.1   Interactive communications model

Noise can also be defined as jargon or slang that is not readily understood by both sides; attitudinal noise in which the speakers have an emotional disconnect through a disagreement, frustration, or severe difference of opinion also is noise. Again, while the individuals may be able to hear each other clearly and even understand the same language, they may have such a strong difference of opinion that the message will not get through.

As marketers one of our biggest challenges in any marketplace is to do whatever we can to reduce the amount of noise between our message delivery system (advertising) and the recipient of our message (the consumer). As you can see from our model, one of the things that allows us to bypass the noise is a secondary level of communication we call feedback. Feedback is best defined as a secondary level of communication or messaging that allows senders to alter their messages so that they do a better job of bypassing noise.

For example, when trying to communicate in a noisy environment, the receiver might indicate to the sender that the message is not coming through by putting a hand to his/her ear or beckoning the sender closer. This simple feedback loop sends a second message to indicate that the first message was not effectively received.

Feedback loops can include many aspects of human body language, facial expressions, sounds, comments, and other cues that tell us whether or not our messages are being delivered.

What does this model look like using traditional marketing channels? Well, for starters the feedback loop is almost totally missing. Certainly, consumers provide a level of feedback when they vote with their wallets, but it's very difficult for most advertisers to determine the specific impact of a campaign merely by looking at sales receipts. The long and short answer is that unless people are willing to dial an 800 number or to send a letter in some form to the company, there is very little feedback in most traditional marketing channels. And no, yelling at your television doesn't count.

This means that most Goliath advertisers have to depend on very good planning or sheer luck to know whether they are effectively bypassing the layer of noise between themselves and their target consumers. Not only that, there are very few ways to measure whether a message was received by consumers and what they intend to do with that new information or understanding.

But what if we take this model and position it in an interactive environment such as the web? Because everything that is done online by consumers is done on purpose, we can measure the points of interaction between consumers and the brand messaging in online ads, landing pages, web links, or any other point of contact between brands and consumers.

By creating feedback mechanisms (for example, measuring the number of people who click on an ad in order to calculate that ad's click-through rate), we can get a better sense of how an ad was received, understood, and acted upon. We can also create tools and opportunities to allow consumers to react and communicate directly, through use of questions, comments, frustrations, pleasantries, and any other aspect that brings our marketing models closer to more real-world interpersonal communication models.

The bottom line is that people communicate like people whether they are online or not. Because today's consumers understand that they now have a voice in the online marketplace, they expect to be able to communicate directly with advertisers and publishers. They expect to share their opinions and thoughts. They expect to be able to ask questions and have direct access to someone providing them with information. This is not a small point and should not be ignored. To be effective in today's online marketplace marketers have to be fully present and make themselves available as the other side of the conversation they are having with consumers.

Effectively delivering a message is only a small part of this model. Even more important is having something to say that the people receiving the message want to hear.

UNDERSTANDING THE MESSAGE

As marketers, our primary job is to shift consumers' perception so that in the future they will act differently.

While we use different channels to communicate with consumers, it is not the channels themselves that make this communication happen. It's the message we send through these channels that makes the difference. And it's not simply the process of tossing a few words on an ad banner or sending out an e-mail that makes a campaign effective. It's about starting a meaningful and personally relevant conversation with consumers who have a problem they need solved.

This also means that just because a consumer sees or interacts with an ad we know that the message was received. In order for the message to find a home, it needs to meet a personal point of relevancy with the consumer. We've all experienced years and years of advertising that wasn't relevant to us personally. Even if we understood the language and the message, there was no place for that ad in our lives. In short, our intentions to use that message to help us make an informed buying decision in the future never took place. For any advertising to be effective, it has to shift the consumer's perception toward one of taking future action.

For example, most consumers who live in the United States are familiar with the Ford truck brand. Because we have been exposed to Ford truck ads for many years, most of us can readily identify a Ford truck, understand some of the benefits and features it offers, and know how we might go about buying one. But unless Ford advertising is able to create in the consumers they reach a desire and need to buy a Ford truck now or in the future, then the campaign fundamentally fails because its success isn't really about reaching the greatest number of people as many times as possible. After all, Ford is in the business of selling trucks and not of merely talking about them.

Creating meaningful and relevant messages is based on meeting the emotional needs of the consumers who receive them. These needs are often very personal, and they are also generally subconscious and are directly related to the pain and pleasure principles.

UNDERSTANDING HUMAN PERCEPTION FILTERS

In order to communicate with people, we need to understand how they see the world and how that perception affects their behavior.

Whenever we communicate with other people, there is an additional layer of noise we need to get through in the form of personal cognitive filters. These are filters that control what information gets into our heads and what doesn't. These filters are based on our personal experiences, likes, dislikes, and perceptions of the world around us. Basically, if we don't think we like something, aren't receptive to it, or don't find it personally relevant, then it isn't getting in.

There are two types of cognitive filters:

1. Relevancy filters
2. Comfort filters

As you might imagine, relevancy filters have to do with whether a message matches the current need or understanding or solves a specific problem in the consumer's mind. Relevancy is all about meeting personal needs. These needs depend on consumers' understanding and consideration of the message and considering whether that message clearly allows consumers to see how the value or benefit of an offer can be directly applied to meeting their needs.

For example, trying to sell a large slice of cheese pizza to a person who is highly lactose intolerant is never going to meet personal relevancy needs no matter how you position it. There's just no connection to be made here. On the other hand, a consumer with a car that is becoming less and less reliable is going to find offers for a new vehicle more and more relevant every day. As consumers move toward a new mindset and understanding, the relevancy of messages catering to that need or understanding increases.

And this brings us to the idea of timeliness—timeliness is associated with how relevant a message is at a point in time. For example, let's say that a friend calls you up one evening and invites you out to dinner. If you have not yet had your evening meal, this offer would be very relevant to your current needs. However, if you have just returned from eating your dinner in a local diner before you received the call, then chances are good that you will be taking a rain check on the offer.

The same thing holds true for consumers who have their relevant needs met. Let's use the example of a person looking to buy a new car again. As the need for a more reliable automobile grows, the consumer will start to tune into the idea of buying a replacement car. He or she will start to see car ads everywhere, almost as though by magic, and will use what the information gained to make a decision. However, once that decision has been made and the consumer drives away in a new car, then that need simply vanishes. A car ad presented the day after the purchase will simply fall on deaf ears and blind eyes. It is no longer relevant.

The comfort filters have more to do with how we interact with the channels that deliver marketing messages. These filters include concepts such as ease of use, ease of assimilation, fear avoidance, empowerment, and engagement. The long and short of the comfort filters is that if the process of receiving information through ads, web pages, landing pages, e-mails, search engines, or any other channel is confusing or difficult in any way, most consumers will react by avoiding that content as part of their pain avoidance mechanism. *Nobody* likes to feel incapable or stupid.

While we won't go into greater detail in this book regarding comfort filters, we will explore best practices for each of the digital marketing channels we cover to help you better understand ways to position content and messaging so that it doesn't get filtered out.

CREATING MESSAGES FOR B2C AUDIENCES

Effective marketing is about directly connecting with real people who have real needs and problems they want solved.

In our B2C (business to consumer) messaging matrix we've isolated the following eight areas as strong emotional triggers that consumers rely on to make decisions about the value and benefits of the offers they receive. These are:

- Offers that communicate a sense of well-being
- Offers that communicate a sense of convenience
- Offers that communicate a sense of security

- Offers that communicate a sense of productivity/ increased significance
- Offers that communicate a sense of exclusivity
- Offers that communicate a sense of continuity
- Offers that communicate a sense of positive social standing
- Offers that communicate a sense of possibility

Note that each of these triggers is about allowing the person at the other end of the exchange to sense something. Because human beings are highly emotional, these messages are often delivered subconsciously but still trigger consumers' emotions. Note that each one of these triggers gets back to the core human need of seeking pleasure and avoiding pain.

Whenever we create a new campaign, we start by trying to gain a better understanding of what our target customers need to know or understand in order to be persuaded to take future action. We often start by asking ourselves in what way the message we create will best resonate with our target audience and why? Which emotions should it trigger? How can we best tie the specific uses of a product to different emotional triggers, and how can those be used to drive awareness and eventual conversion?

Before we explore the how, let's better define the parameters of these emotional triggers:

Offers That Communicate a Sense of Well-Being

Most people want to feel good about themselves and their lives. They want to believe that the products and services they buy will help them do just that. This emotional trigger is a broad category that can relate to food and eating, health care, leisure activities, philanthropic activities, entertainment, wellness, comfort, love, relationships with other people, and relationships with brands.

In short, any product or service that helps consumers feel good about themselves fits into this category.

Offers That Communicate a Sense of Convenience

One of the commodities we use to measure the quality of our lives is how we spend our time. We understand that we have limited time not only during the average day but throughout our lives. We also understand that we have obligations that, while necessary, are often points of discomfort and eat into our time. As a result, people often look for things that will free up their time and allow them to do things faster, more easily, and more affordably.

Products and services that cater to a sense of convenience can include time-saving devices, new solutions for existing problems, and faster access to solutions. For example, eating at a restaurant may cost more than preparing a similar meal at home, but the convenience of not having to prepare the meal and clean up after is worth the price difference to many people. This time savings allows us to get to the pleasurable part of the process (the dining experience and the eating of the food) while avoiding the less desirable attributes (cooking and cleaning).

Offers That Communicate a Sense of Security

Human beings are wired for self-preservation. We will do whatever we can to protect ourselves physically and emotionally. That includes paying attention to our health and safety, our financial future, and our emotional states. Products and services that relate to security include insurance, financial investing, collectibles, safety devices, emergency items, and personal protection.

A message that helps consumers minimize fear while providing them with a way to secure themselves resonates very well with people looking for a sense of security.

Offers That Communicate a Sense of Productivity/ Increased Significance

People like to feel that they're making progress and reaching their goals. They want to feel that they are accomplishing something of meaning through their time and efforts. Products and services that help meet these needs include educational materials, time-saving devices, mental or physical enhancements, convenience products, and services that minimize less desirable or repetitive tasks such as housekeeping, laundry, food preparation, or even shopping.

People looking to feel more productive, effective, or significant will be looking for products and services that can help them free up time and allow them to use the time they save to accomplish things of greater personal importance.

Offers That Communicate a Way to Feel Special/Advantaged

While most people feel most comfortable going along with the crowd, in certain circumstances they do want to stand out. People like to feel unique and special. They like the idea of being part of an exclusive group. They like to be part of something that's bigger than they are. The desire to feel special and advantaged may be hardwired. Very few of us have a desire to be "ordinary."

Products and services that cater to meeting this need include limited-time offers, members-only offers, personalized products, luxury products, and even being an early adopter of advanced technologies that can help us stand out from the crowd.

Offers That Communicate a Sense of Continuity

As a general rule, people don't like change. Most people like to maintain a certain sense of balance in their lives. This means that they are receptive to opportunities that allow continuity of events or services in their lives.

Continuity can be related to services such as automatic bill paying, renewing magazine subscriptions, regularly scheduled home cleaning, or care services such as insurance, replacement contracts, or warranties for products purchased.

Offers That Communicate a Sense of Positive Social Standing

For most people, their perceived level of community or social standing is very important. People need to belong to groups of other people, and within those groups they need to establish and maintain a certain level of status.

Marketing opportunities relating to the need for social standing include fashion, cosmetics, educational materials, health, self-improvement tools for both mind and body, and luxury items.

Offers That Communicate a Sense of Possibility

While we need to live in the present, many of us are constantly thinking about ways to create a better future.

Products and services that relate to a sense of possibility include education programs and materials, investments, travel opportunities, and lottery, sweepstakes, and gambling. Even this book represents a sense of possibility for marketers who expect that by reading and understanding the knowledge we're sharing they will be able to create a better future for themselves (and this assumption is absolutely correct!).

POSITIONING MESSAGES

Now that we know what the offer is and how it may be approached emotionally by consumers, the next step is to ask ourselves how the product or service offered can affect any or all of those emotional states.

In most cases, an offer is going to find a good connection with at least one of these emotional states; many offers will be able to take advantage of more than one. For example, let's say a manufacturer of a backyard jungle gym/swing set is looking to create marketing messages that will better resonate with the emotional needs of its target audience—parents. For a product like this, a marketer could create several significant connections between these emotional needs and communicate how this product can meet those needs. For example, this type of product offer can:

Communicate a sense of well-being. Most parents want to do well by their children. Being able to give their children access to something that allows them to get some fresh air and stay fit through exercise will give most parents a sense of well-being.

Communicate a sense of convenience. With a playground in your own backyard you no longer need to be inconvenienced by trips to the community playground. Your children can play at their convenience without impacting your schedule.

Communicate a sense of security. When your children play in their own yard, they have less exposure to strangers or social challenges and can experience an increased sense of security.

Communicate a sense of productivity/increased significance. Because you don't need to take your children someplace else to play, you will free up time to get more done at home. Because of the increased convenience and security considerations, you will free up even more time!

Communicate a sense of exclusivity. Not everybody can afford to have a playground in the backyard. Good for you that you can!

Communicate a sense of positive social standing. Not only are your children benefitting from easy access to their own private playground, but other children in the neighborhood are going to notice what you have and either encourage their parents to get a playground for them or start becoming frequent visitors to your backyard and in turn make your home a social and community destination point.

This is a single product that can communicate many different messages that can relate to many different needs. How would you create messages for the products and services you and your company market?

Take a moment to look over the message targeting matrix. Which of the emotional triggers can you address? Can you identify how your message will meet the emotional needs of consumers?

THE B2B MESSAGE TARGETING MATRIX

Meeting the emotional needs of consumers can give marketers a direct path toward formulating their messages.

In a B2B context, the people we communicate with are not necessarily buying for themselves or people emotionally close to them. It's worth pointing out that we are still communicating directly with other people but the criteria used to persuade people are different on this side of the fence.

For starters, many of the problems business buyers are trying to solve are different from those consumers and personal buyers deal with. There is also an additional element in the B2B relationship in that the persons making the purchase decision is also concerned about how the decision may reflect back upon them professionally. That is, many decision makers are very cautious about making decisions that might affect their jobs.

The B2B message targeting matrix focuses on asking questions that shift the perception of how the proposed solution is going to benefit a company or business.

As with the B2C targeting matrix, our research has helped us create six questions, the answers to which can help B2B marketers better define and isolate meaningful marketing messages so they can better meet the needs of corporate customers. When marketers approach the market as if they are solutions looking for problems, they often do a better job of finding where those opportunities are.

The questions we ask to home in on the best B2B messages are as follows:

- How does this solution help solve existing business problems?
- How does this solution help provide a sense of competitive advantage?
- How does this solution help the company to be seen as visionary/ market leader?
- How does this solution show that it is an obvious value exchange?
- How does this solution show that it represents an exclusive opportunity for business?
- How does this solution increase performance and productivity?

Of course, once answers are selected, it's important that marketers outline how the solution can deliver this answer or solution.

How Does this Solution Help Solve Existing Business Problems?

All businesses face daily challenges that affect their sales efforts, the manufacturing efforts, their human resources and recruitment efforts, their physical plant efforts, and any other thing that keeps the business viable and profitable.

As with the B2C matrix, solutions that minimize or make these problems go away are appealing to other people. Not only can solving the problem benefit the company as a whole but for the individuals who are responsible for fixing the problem there are emotional benefits.

How Does this Solution Help Provide a Sense of Competitive Advantage?

Many companies spend a great deal of time thinking about the threats they face from competitors in their marketplace. Solutions that can minimize those threats are very appealing. Also, solutions that can turn a threat into an opportunity are equally enticing.

In a world where the common scenario is "eat or be eaten" being able to help companies to be better predators and less likely to be prey can be compelling.

How Does this Solution Help the Company to be Seen as Visionary/Market Leader?

Part of the competitive advantage in the marketplace is being perceived by that market as a leader in some way. In our careers we've worked on many campaigns with clients who want to be seen as thought leaders or market leaders. Every company should be striving to find an identity that helps it to extend its unique selling proposition—whatever it is that helps the company to stand out from the crowd for good reasons. Solutions that provide businesses with this opportunity are greatly appealing.

How Does this Solution Show that it is an Obvious Value Exchange?

Smart companies are always looking for return on investment. The bottom line is that if you're going to spend time, money, or other resources on finding a solution, then that solution should pay for itself.

Solutions that save companies time and money are great examples of value exchange. Solutions that empower employees through advanced understanding or better use of existing resources are also good examples of value exchange. New equipment or procedures that make jobs more efficient, easier, and even safer are also good examples.

How Does this Solution Show that it Represents an Exclusive Opportunity for Business?

In the business world exclusivity isn't just a social ego boost but can represent a significant competitive advantage. Companies that have access to or can sell products and services not available to their competitors can position themselves better in the marketplace. Also, like people, businesses like to be known for what sets them apart from other businesses. Exclusivity may be appealing because it automatically provides businesses with a competitive advantage.

How Does this Solution Increase Performance and Productivity?

Companies that are more efficient and use their time, money, and other resources most effectively also have a better shot at being more profitable. Solutions that provide increased performance through equipment or personnel upgrades, new approaches to manufacturing and distribution, and an increase in productivity can all meet this need.

HOW TO POSITION THE B2B MESSAGE

Let's say that you're a distributor for a winery. Your job is to sell cases of wine to restaurants in your area. Obviously, the more wine you sell, the more profit your company makes. But in order to work with local restaurants, the benefit you offer has to be about them and not you. So, let's take a look at some of the solutions you can provide to your prospects:

Does your solution help solve existing business problems? Again, businesses are in business to make money. If your price point for a bottle of wine allows restaurants to tack on a significant markup, then every bottle of wine they sell allows them to make money.

Does your solution help provide a sense of competitive advantage? For a restaurant that wants to be known for its fine dining, being able to pair unique and exclusive wines with the meals they serve could be a significant competitive advantage. As a distributor, you may choose to sell your wines only through specialty or high-end restaurants and may actually limit the number of restaurants in an area that sell your wines in order to give these businesses that competitive advantage.

Does your solution show that it is an obvious value exchange? Again, if your price point between the retail sale of a bottle of wine and the price the restaurant can sell that wine for are significant, then yes, there is an obvious value exchange in place.

Different consumers have different needs. Different businesses have different needs. The people who make decisions in the companies they work for are continuously looking for cues that will help them find solutions to problems. While the problems don't have to be overly dramatic or significant, they are still real needs that need to be met.

The message you deliver to your prospects and customers should be in line with their needs and desires. Even if you have the best marketing distribution in place if the message doesn't resonate with the recipient, then the campaign won't work. As marketers, our goal is to create the perfect combination of audience, message, and distribution.

As we will explore throughout the remainder of this book, there are plenty of ways we can try to get the right message to the right person at the right time, but no single channel can do it alone.

CHAPTER 5

DIGITAL DISPLAY ADVERTISING

Digital display ads are the core of online advertising. They are also one of the most misused digital advertising tools.

When we talk about digital display advertising, we can either look at it from the perspective of what channel to choose or from a strategic perspective. Digital display advertising generally refers to banner ads, but in the larger scheme of things there are several different types of digital display advertising approaches, such as:

- Rich media ads
- Text ads
- Contextual search ads
- Sponsorships
- Advertorials/native ads
- Social media ads

The different ad units pretty much offer a similar process for bringing advertisers and consumers together. For the sake of this book, we're going to classify digital display ads as ads that serve the purpose of offering consumers a link that when clicked on will take consumers to a place where they can learn more about an offer.

We're going to toss down the cheerleading pom-poms for a moment and take a cold, hard look at digital display advertising. The reality is that it's a hot mess. There are articles and studies showing up almost daily talking about how the majority of digital ad impressions are never even seen by a human being. Add to that the poor response rates for most digital ads (somewhere generally in the range of .03 percent to .05 percent for click-through rates, which translates to 0.3 to 0.5 clicks every 1,000 times an ad is shown; this isn't stellar) and you've got something that seems to have run off its rails a long time ago.

But like any other marketing channel or tool, digital display advertising is based upon best practices for ad placement and for creative design as well as on making sure that the conversation started in the ad space gets continued on the landing page. As we will explore, there is plenty of opportunity for misuse and mayhem.

We like the potential of digital display advertising. What we hate is how it is often misused and misunderstood by advertisers.

Strategically, display ads have faced some pretty tough odds over the past two decades. Many early online advertisers erroneously thought that web advertising was pretty much a slam dunk for success and that placing ads on sites around the web would allow consumers to click on them, drive traffic to landing pages, and make gobs of money for the advertisers.

It didn't exactly turn out that way.

Instead, early advertisers often faced the frustration of not being able to control where their ads ran and who saw them. Instead, they needed to rely on the publishers and ad networks they worked with to make sure that their ads got in front of the right people at the right time. In most cases that didn't happen.

Coupled with weak ad placement was the challenge that web ads were still a form of "interrupt" advertising that required consumers to choose between the content on the pages they were visiting and the ads on those pages. In most cases this wasn't much of a contest. The model was further weakened after consumers became more familiar with the model and started to experience huge disconnects between the offer being made in the ad space and the offer being offered on the landing page. Pop-up ads, which were designed to do a better job of grabbing consumers' attention, generally also raised the ire of most consumers and painted a very negative picture of web advertising in general.

This meant that after the novelty of early banner advertising had worn off, consumers settled into their new roles as captains of their online destinies and were happily navigating their way around the web without ever needing to directly interact with advertising.

Does this mean that digital display advertising doesn't work? No, it doesn't. But it does mean that there's a lot more that goes into planning and creating digital display ad campaigns than just throwing a few banner ads up on a web page or two. Effective digital display advertising is about understanding how to communicate value to consumers when they are online so that they will be inspired to get involved. Not surprisingly, web advertising isn't that much different from the strategies that traditional advertisers have used for years to try to get the attention of consumers. That is, they have to create an opportunity to talk with consumers directly and then make offers that are relevant, meaningful, and timely.

THE EVOLUTION OF BANNER AD ADVERTISING AND AD SERVING

Digital display advertising started from some pretty humble roots. Like most things, it got better over time.

As we explored in chapter 1, the first ad banner almost accidentally ushered in the age of online advertising. The ad size itself was arbitrary (measuring 468 $\times$ 60 pixels in size because that was the size of the hole the ad was filling on the hotwired.com page), but because it came first, those measurements became the first standard for banner ads. That first ad wasn't animated or offered any kind of secondary function. It was a simple graphic (and a fairly unattractive one at that!) the purpose of which was simply to serve as a link between the publisher's site and the advertiser's site.

But as poorly designed and arbitrary as this ad may have been, it was also the first online ad campaign to go viral. World spread quickly across the web about this new approach to advertising, and advertisers and publishers both sat up and took notice. The result was a click-through rate in the 30 percent range and the ushering in of what would grow to be a multibillion industry less than 20 years later.

The early days of banner advertising may have been heady, but they weren't very robust. For example, the earliest banner ad campaigns were not served to web pages but needed to be hardwired into those pages by site IT departments and webmasters. This meant that early ads were not sold based on the number of impressions that would be served over time but based on time itself. In many instances the agreements between early web advertisers and publishers were based on the amount of time, the weeks and months, a banner would stay on that page.

While this early solution gave publishes a way to sell advertisers space on their web pages and sites, this was not a scalable approach. It was also difficult to control who saw the ads, how many times any ad was shown to any particular consumer, or what the overall impact of the campaign was.

Over time, the technology of ad serving was born. This allowed publishers to add code to their pages that would allow those pages to get content from other computers and servers when a page loaded. This meant that hardwiring ads directly into pages was out, and publishers could now offer advertisers a place in the advertising queue. Now every time a web page loaded, the ad position could be filled with a different piece of creative. This meant that publishers could work with more advertisers (and make more money) and that advertisers could have more flexibility regarding where and when their ads were seen.

Because advertisers were still buying web space directly from publishers, this also led to a bit of a landgrab. Because much of the media buying was contextually driven, popular categories, such as automotive, experienced terrible growing pains. For example, it's not much of a surprise that automotive manufacturers or resellers would want to get their messages in front of people who like cars and may be looking to buy one. The natural approach for this strategy is to buy space on web sites that cater to car information, reviews of new models, and aftermarket modifications. It's also not much of a stretch to consider that automotive marketing managers worth their salary would tap into the same handful of highly targeted sites to get the job done. Unfortunately, this meant that there was always limited ad inventory on these sites (which didn't make the publishers unhappy at all), and the competition and pricing were fierce. The result was that automotive advertisers were often shut out of the markets they most wanted to reach because supply could not keep up with market demand.

This overwhelming demand also caught the attention of publishers who could see how much money was being left on the table. As a result, many of them attempted to create more inventory by increasing the page count of their web sites. They built microsites and alternative landing pages. They created sponsorship pages or new content pages that ran articles. This increased the number of ads they could display at any given time and took care of the backlog of advertisers still trying to get a seat at the table. Then as a result of a weakened global economy and the sudden shift in the balance between supply and demand, the price of inventory took a nose-dive and now publishers were dealing with an abundance of inventory they needed to sell and fewer advertisers who wanted it. This resulted in inventory fire sales across the web and the sleazy and opportunistic marketers moved in.

DISPLAY ADVERTISING BEST PRACTICES

Best practices for any industry are often best developed by first watching companies do a dreadful job with their first attempts.

While we don't want to necessarily focus on things that don't work in a channel, it's worth taking a moment to explore a few digital display advertising strategies that are poor choices so that we can eventually focus on those that work.

Let's slaughter a few sacred cows:

- While click-through rates can be easily measured, it's generally a weak metric and one that tells a very limited story. Savvy marketers focus on defining and measuring conversion instead.
- No matter how well thought out or engaging a campaign is if the creatives aren't shown to the right people, then it's a practically

useless undertaking. Savvy marketers understand the importance of creating well-targeted campaigns and then doing whatever they can to get those ads in front of that target audience.

- While getting consumers to click on an ad might be considered important, what takes place after the click is *very* important. Savvy marketers design and create targeted landing pages for their campaigns that effectively extend the offer being made in the ad space and work to turn an interest into a point of conversion. We will take a much closer look at the strategies behind meaningful landing page design and uses later in this chapter.

- While getting people to engage with ads is important, that engagement needs to be meaningful and lead to another phase of communication or understanding on the part of the consumer. Savvy marketers are always thinking about how they can create meaningful relationships with the consumers they do reach. This holds true for both Davids and Goliaths.

So here are a few strategic takeaways to start with:

- *Always* define why the campaign is being created in the first place and then figure out how you're going to measure whether those goals are being met. If the campaign is to promote a brand, then how will you know whether brand uplift is taking place? If it's a direct response campaign, then how are you measuring meaningful response? Hint: it has nothing to do with click-through rates!

- If you expect to have a meaningful conversation with consumers you first need to have an understanding of what they want and need and where they're going to be. Talking to people who don't care about what you're offering isn't that much different from sharing the campaign with a dog except that the dog might be polite enough to stick around for a while.

- Online conversations are very similar to real-world conversations. This means that if you interrupt people, are boring, are irrelevant, or act rude, then you're going to be largely ignored. Instead, figure out what you can do to be meaningfully engaging, bring value to consumers, and help them find solutions to their problems. We're serious here. If you can figure out ways to treat your prospects like friends you want to help, then you're going to be much more popular and will be invited to more parties than you probably were in high school.

DEVELOPMENT OF BEST STRATEGIES FOR DISPLAY ADVERTISING CAMPAIGNS

Effective digital display advertising requires strong audience targeting strategies to be successful.

While the fundamentals of audience targeting, refining a message, and selecting the right channels are all part of any successful campaign, the initial step that needs to be taken before anything else matters is to find an effective way to attract consumers' attention and communicate with them about the personal benefits of an offer.

There are a number of different approaches advertisers can take when designing and creating display ads. Here are five fundamental strategies that every ad must incorporate in order to be effective:

Strategy # 1: Offer Consumers a Strong Benefit Statement

Most web ads are seriously restricted by the amount of space they have to tell a compelling story. Instead, they almost necessarily need to rely on a come-on in order to create enough allure to cause consumers to click on the ad even if only to satisfy their curiosity.

The biggest consideration for any advertiser hoping to meaningfully reach consumers is based on clearly communicating to consumers what benefits and values are being offered.

There's an old line that says that the average consumer's favorite radio station is WII-FM—what's in it for me? This isn't to say that human beings are vastly selfish, but the reality is that we all spend 24/7 in our own heads.

Figure 5.1   Benefit statements and calls to action

As a result, our environment is determined by those things that are most personally relevant. We look for images and for keywords; we look for things that we recognize. We look for our own names and the names of products that are already familiar. We are continuously trying to answer the question "what's in this for me?" We are all about ourselves and our own interests.

A strong benefit statement is just that; it tells consumers why they should care. It tells them that it's worth taking a moment to pay attention because a strong value and personal benefit await them.

Benefit statements don't need to be grandiose. They simply need to communicate why consumers should stop paying attention to everything else on the page and pay attention to the ad instead. As you can see from the ads in figure 5.1, a benefit statement can be very simple and to the point.

Strategy # 2: Include a Strong Call to Action to Move Consumers Forward

When we see things in our world that mesh with our existing needs and interests, we are open to receiving more understanding. Often, we subconsciously want to know what we need to do to receive the benefit being offered. Understanding this is a very important part of how to further engage online consumers.

A call to action is just that. It's an indication, statement, or cue that explains to consumers what they need to do next. In studies that have measured campaign interaction results of ads offering a clear call to action and those without, the results have consistently shown that without clear instructions fewer consumers will react at all even if the benefit offered is relevant and meaningful.

As with benefit statements, calls to action don't have to be overly complex. They simply need to point out what consumers should do next to get the desired results. Once again, creating compelling messages doesn't take deep pockets. Advertisers who keep an eye on the needs and interests of their prospects have an advantage here. What matters is being innovative, understanding your market, and keeping an eye on your goals.

Strategy #3: Ads Should Lead to a Targeted/ Relevant Landing Page when Clicked on

As we discussed in chapter 2, accurately measuring conversion results of a campaign is the most important part of the campaign. When we think of the relationship between an ad and a landing page, we want to think of a partnership where the ad is responsible for attracting consumers' attention and starting the conversation, and the landing page is designed to continue that conversation and further the understanding of the benefits and values of the campaign.

But the landing page is also where the conversion happens.

In earlier days, the majority of advertisers simply drove traffic to the home pages of their websites. While this certainly would allow consumers to arrive at a destination that might provide them with more insight, in most cases consumers were left on their own to explore and to see if they could pick up the same conversation that the advertisers had started with them in the ad space. In a lot of ways it's like inviting people to a party at your house and then leaving them on the front stoop when they arrive.

Driving traffic to a vague destination is a wasted opportunity. In most cases meaningful conversion won't occur because consumers will follow the path of least resistance.

As a best practice you will want to create landing pages that are the fraternal twin of the ad. This means that while they are different pieces of media with different goals and objectives, they are interrelated and need to work together to create a consistent and meaningful experience for consumers. If an ad makes an offer or presents a proposition, then once consumers click on it, the resulting landing page should reflect and address those same messages and elements.

Unfortunately, there are many terrible examples of interrelationships between ads and landing pages. From lapses in design that make it seem as though the ad and landing page are from separate campaigns to messages that come on strong in the ad and are totally missing on the landing page, a poor interrelationship between these campaign elements can leave consumers disconnected and very confused.

Despite bad planning, we can assume that the click through rates for an ad are going to be fairly low to begin with, based on industry averages. But add to that a campaign that has a huge disconnect between the message in the ad and the message on the landing page and those few clicks are going to end up being wasted if they can't lead toward conversion goals. However, creative that starts a conversation in the ad space and effectively continues it on the landing page is taking full advantage of the media and the medium.

There is another strong consideration when designing landing pages that also harkens back to the need for tight conversion parameters. Every campaign should have an identifiable point of conversion. This should be only one thing that gets measured to determine the effectiveness of a campaign. This means that if traffic is being driven to a landing page, then that landing page should be precisely aligned with the conversion goals of the campaign.

Strategy #4: Ads Should be Targeted to Audiences

One basic tenet of digital advertising is that one size does not fit all. Unlike more old-school mass marketing models, digital advertising is a one-person-at-a-time marketing model. Not only isn't it a mass event, but every online consumer who sees a link or an ad does so in a unique context.

When we create web ads, we often have a specific target audience in mind. To that point, it's not much of a hardship to create additional ad units that address the specific needs, understandings, identities, or desires of the specific audience segments. It's easy to change design colors, benefit statements, and calls to action to better communicate with specific audience segments. A simple example would be a campaign that sells cell phone services and creates different ads for millennial prospects, business prospects, and recent retiree prospects. While the services being offered to all three groups might be largely identical, how those group perceive the offer will not be the same. The bottom line is that different ad creative can do a better job reaching the specific needs and interests of each group and can start a more meaningful conversation with each using each segment's language.

A simple example of this might be advertisers selling running shoes. Instead of creating a generic one-size-fits-all ad for their running shoes and showing it all over the web, the advertisers would get greater traction by creating multiple ad units that focus on different aspects of the products they offer and on the different types of people who buy those products. For example, an ad that caters to running shoes for men should be different and have a different focus than an ad that offers running shoes for women. While the shoes may be fundamentally the same, the perception from the consumers' standpoint is that most men aren't going to pay attention to an offer selling shoes for women and vice versa. In this example, the advertisers might also think about the different ways in which their shoes are used by consumers and create campaign elements that address the needs of distance runners, CrossFit aficionados, and people just looking for a comfortable pair of athletic shoes to wear at the gym.

The bottom line is that different people buy for different reasons. By creating multiple ads and focusing them on slightly different audience segments, advertisers can find more traction because the solutions they are providing are more relevant to the various groups.

Strategy # 5: Multiple Creatives Should Always be Run During a Campaign

As we mentioned in the preceding section, creating multiple variations of ads to address the different audience needs is incredibly important. It's also important to create different variations of a single ad that can run throughout the life of a campaign. In many cases, these variations are merely small tweaks that offer similar benefit statements but differ visually.

For example, let's say that advertisers are creating a skyscraper ad unit as part of an upcoming campaign. Let's also say that the media buy is going to be for 1,000,000 impressions over a 30-day period.

This type of media buy isn't that unusual. But what the advertisers may not be taking into consideration is that during the month that the ad is running on the site, it may be seen by a lot of the same people over and over again. This means that over time the visual impact of the ad, and in turn its message, are going to become less and less significant to many of the site's visitors. If we were to measure this ad over time, we would undoubtedly see a consistent decline in ad interaction during the life of the campaign. We refer to this as banner burnout, and it's not something that most advertisers want to have happen.

Now let's say that instead of a single ad creative for that position, the advertiser creates four different ads. Each ad is similar to the others but presents slightly different messages, color combinations, images, etc. This time, instead of running a single ad for 30 days, the advertiser runs each ad for 7 days. Now if we were to measure the interaction rates across the campaign, we would generally see an increase in ad interaction rates every week as the new ad comes online. If the general message between all variations of the ad is similar enough, all the ads could even point to the same landing page.

Creating multiple ads is often the least expensive part of an ad campaign. While it requires more management of individual ad units, having designers create multiple variations of ads is well worth any extra cost as it will generally create a much higher yield and conversion rate than those campaigns that stick to a limited ad and creative run.

FOCUS ON RICH MEDIA ADVERTISING

Rich media ads stand out from the crowd because they offer dynamic and engaging features not found in other digital display ad models.

Rich media ads are defined as ads that offer a level of interactivity beyond that of a simple click-through. In fact, rich media ads often don't even require a click-through at all because they can grab attention, feature a call to action, and serve as the landing page all in one!

The features and functions common to rich media ad formats include the ability to expand, capture data, play videos, print documents, download digital items, and use tools. In essence, most rich media ads are landing pages in themselves embedded in a publisher's web page. This means that instead of focusing on getting consumers to click on an ad during the time the ad is presented to them, rich media ad formats can instead focus on persuading consumers to reach points of conversion within the ad unit. This approach largely eliminates the need to measure click-through rates at all and increases campaign results fairly dramatically in most cases as consumers are able to explore and interact with a brand message without needing to make a decision to leave the page the ad is on.

Because rich media ad units are self-contained marketing and sales tools, there are ways they can be measured that dramatically overshadow the metrics of most traditional digital display ads. Not only can ad units measure for clicks on different definable elements within an ad (such as buttons and other interactive features), but rich media ads can also measure time of engagement data, such as how long a consumer's cursor hovers over the ad space and specific elements within the ad. These simple metrics often translate into solid brand awareness and brand uplift data using the reasoning that the longer a consumer is engaged, the better the branding opportunity.

Perhaps more important, points of direct conversion can be measured within the ad unit. This means that if the conversion goal is to collect e-mail address data or to have consumers print a document or download a digital file or watch a video, each point of interaction can be easily tracked and measured to help determine the campaign's overall success.

Finally, rich media ads can be used to help brands do market research while a campaign is running. For example, if an automotive manufacturer created an ad that profiled three different new car models and an invitation for consumers to simply roll over each model to learn more about its features, then apart from driving brand awareness, the data from those interactions could be used to see which models were getting the most attention. In turn, the advertisers could then use that insight to create ads that focused more tightly on those models and features.

While offering huge advantages over most digital display banner ads, rich media ads are also harder to create and more expensive to produce. Most rich media ad formats also need to be served by special ad serving companies so that they can be "wired" properly to allow for interactions to be measured. All that said, rich media advertising remains a powerful way to attract consumers' attention, tell a compelling story, and reach points of conversion all in one place.

STRATEGIES FOR LANDING PAGE DESIGN AND USE

Good planning and design of digital display ads is paramount, and good landing page design even more so.

Our focus has been on the strategies used to create digital display ads that effectively attract attention, share a message of benefit and value, and then encourage consumers to take further action. In most cases this further action requires a click that will take consumers to a relevant landing page.

We use the word "relevant" almost ironically here because historically there have been too many instances of digital display campaigns that drove traffic straight to advertising home pages or other pages that weren't aligned with the message communicated by the ad.

Practical Wisdom—One bad example of landing page mismatch came from an advertiser who was running ads promoting honeymoon vacation packages. However, when interested consumers clicked through to the landing page for the campaign, they found information about general vacation packages but absolutely nothing about honeymoons. Not only was this a wasted opportunity for the advertiser, but it created a frustrating experience for consumers.

Having a single landing page that caters to multiple facets of an ad campaign is limiting and rarely speaks to the specific needs and interests of consumers. While requiring more resources, a focused and target landing page that can be precisely paired up with ads is a great best practice. The bottom line is that the conversation started in the ad space should continue on the landing page; otherwise, it feels like bait and switch to consumers.

When creating campaigns, you should approach ads and landing pages as two parts of the same conversation. This means that the offer, message, promise, or anything else used to attract consumers' attention should be part of the information consumers find immediately upon clicking on an ad and arriving at the landing page.

In a perfect world every single ad should have a matching landing page. While this isn't always possible considering the number of ads that some campaigns generate, advertisers should be aware that conversion rates will be higher if there is continuity between the ad and the landing page.

While this may sound patently obvious, if you spend a little time clicking on ads to see how well the ad and the landing pages mesh, you're going to quickly discover that few advertisers do a good job linking these parts together. The bottom line is that your campaign is already going to have a low click-through rate. If you end up squandering those few opportunities for conversion because you don't think through the consumers' experience, then you are absolutely wasting a great opportunity as well as plenty of money and time.

This means that if you create a variation of the ad to reflect a specific offer or to target a specific audience, the landing page should also be adapted so that there are no disconnects. This includes design elements such as fonts, colors, and layouts.

As we have discussed in previous chapters, focusing on and accurately measuring conversion is the holy grail of all advertising. When designing landing pages, it's equally important to define the points of conversion and then focus the campaign's full attention on reaching the conversion goal.

For example, let's say that the goal of the campaign is to drive traffic to a landing page where visitors can leave their e-mail address in exchange for the opportunity to download a new e-book. In this case, the conversion goal is defined precisely, and in the best-case scenario consumers would be driven to this page, and the only thing this page would allow consumers to do is exactly what it was set out to do, namely, to leave their e-mail address and hit a submit button.

Unfortunately, a number of advertisers use a Swiss-Army-knife approach to their landing pages and give visitors in some cases dozens of links they can click on once they arrived at that page. This opens up the door for consumers to get lost in the weeds and for advertisers to miss their conversion opportunity.

The bottom line is that the landing page design and message focus should not be an afterthought. It should be planned and designed as part of the campaign. Perhaps even more important, there should be many variations of each landing page in play so that advertisers can do effective multivariate testing of the campaign. By having different landing pages to work with, advertisers can measure conversion success among the various pages and more quickly identify those pages that contribute to a higher conversion rate.

CHAPTER 6

TACTICS AND STRATEGIES FOR CREATING EFFECTIVE E-MAIL MARKETING CAMPAIGNS

Despite its quiet and subtle manner, e-mail is a powerhouse of digital marketing potential.

As a marketing tool, e-mail doesn't get a lot of respect. It's not very glamorous and showy; it doesn't have glitzy and cool, cutting-edge features or a "coolest thing since X" buzz. In fact, e-mail doesn't exactly shine like the brightest star because while not everybody uses e-mail as a marketing channel, all of us are recipients of a seemingly endless parade of unwanted, irrelevant, and often distasteful e-mail messages and offers. We've all seen a wide range of misuse and abuse by the less scrupulous marketers among us. What's hiding behind this rather tarnished veneer is one of the most powerful direct response and point-to-point communication tools that has ever been created.

In comparisons of return on investment (ROI) for different marketing channels (online and off-line), e-mail is almost always at the top of the list. E-mail also often ranks at the top as a marketing tool for companies looking to reach a range of business objectives from sales conversion and revenues to building brand awareness and overall lead generation. E-mail also consistently ranks high as a solid way to improve customer retention, qualify leads, support other online marketing programs, and nurture prospects. Add fantastic transactions after the initial sales and follow-up capabilities, and e-mail turns out to be your Swiss Army knife among marketing tools.

According to the Direct Marketing Association (DMA), the average return on investment for e-mail marketing has been between $35 and $40 gross for every dollar invested. Other companies, such as Experian, report that e-mail marketing yields on average an ROI between $.12 and $.14 per e-mail message sent. In short, it's a true money machine. When done right.

While we may sound like cheerleaders regarding e-mail marketing, we like to think that we have a solid reason to cheer. E-mail offers high response rates compared to digital ad banners, search marketing channels, and many social media campaigns. E-mail also offers high click-through rates (averaging 2.4 percent) compared to other channels, such as digital display ad marketing (which offers an industry click-through average of 0.03 percent).

Because e-mail can support other digital media, such as video, audio, and interactive elements, it can be used to create rich and unique points of engagement that are fully measurable. Not only is measurability an important factor for all digital marketing channels and campaigns but in e-mail marketing specifically the ability to do multivariate testing (also known as A/B testing) allows marketers to quickly cultivate the best ways to get the greatest response from a target audience.

Perhaps most important, e-mail marketing creates powerful opportunities for marketers to get their messages in front of people who will not only find the message relevant but, in many cases, have already agreed to receive those messages by opting in and giving their permission. It is estimated that up to one quarter of all e-mail flowing into the average inbox is permission-based commercial messaging.

E-mail is also more cost-effective compared to many other marketing channels. Comparing the cost of more traditional direct mail campaigns to e-mail campaigns shines a bright light on why the onslaught of traditional "junk mail" has declined so dramatically over the past few years. Apart from the cost of copywriting, e-mail layout, and perhaps purchasing qualified e-mail lists, e-mail marketing is virtually free.

Moreover, the technology behind most e-mail programs (also known as mail clients) allows e-mail messages in a variety of formats to easily reach their intended destination. E-mail marketing formats can include straight text, video, audio, and other rich media content.

MEASURING E-MAIL CAMPAIGNS

E-mail marketing's greatest strength is that campaigns can be measured very accurately.

E-mail campaigns can be easily tested and measured to determine ROI and other meaningful campaign metrics, including e-mail deliverability, open rates, interaction rates, interaction with embedded rich media e-mail assets, click-through rates to specific landing pages, and any other types of interactions. These metrics alone offer a wide range of feedback loops that strongly indicate the overall impact, interest, intention, and future engagement potential of a campaign.

E-mail marketing also offers one of the best online marketing laboratories possible when it comes to testing the overall impact and responsiveness of an e-mail message. By creating slightly different variations of an e-mail message, including different subject lines, layouts, graphics, and copywriting formats (also known as multivariate testing), marketers can do a pretty solid apples-to-apples analysis of e-mail campaign elements to gain a better understanding of which factors will best resonate with the target audience.

This means that a marketer with an e-mail list of 100,000 names could choose to send out 10 separate variations of an e-mail message to 10,000 recipients each. This could mean different variations of subject lines, layouts, included media, and overall messaging to each tell a slightly different story to different prospects. Because e-mail campaigns can be executed in hours instead of days or weeks, in less than a day marketers can better define which subject lines, layouts, and other message elements contributed to the highest e-mail open rates, interactivity, and overall click-through and conversion rates. Marketers can then apply what they learn toward future campaign efforts.

Not only does this level of insight make campaigns more effective over time, but it also means that marketers have a lot more flexibility when sending out messages to a target audience on the spur of the moment. This is incredibly important for nonprofit and support organizations that require quick response from their patrons. For example, an organization that deals with disaster relief efforts can get started raising funds even while a natural disaster is still ongoing, and they can start getting money and other support into the right channels as quickly as possible.

Likewise, e-mail messages can be easily tailored to fit seasonal needs, specific holidays, and even weather events. These messages are not only highly relevant and timely for prospects, but they can also serve to create an effective and meaningful brand awareness opportunity for marketers.

THE LEVEL PLAYING FIELD OF E-MAIL MARKETING

In order to be effective as an e-mail marketer, you have to make a direct and personal connection with other people.

Throughout this book we explore how the digital universe has changed the whole marketing and advertising game, and e-mail is a prime example of that. Unlike its predecessor direct mail, e-mail can be delivered in a more timely manner for next to nothing by anybody with a list of e-mail addresses. This means that success is no longer about being a Goliath who has the most cash to sock into a campaign or who can afford to reach the greatest number of people, but instead success is within reach of companies and departments of any size if they focus on finding the best ways to use the channel so that their message best resonates with the recipients.

Based on our personal observations during e-mail campaigns that we have run for our clients, there is no such thing as a perfect e-mail marketing formula that we can turn to. Instead, we need to acknowledge that every campaign is different and unique and is driven by the needs and interests of the people who will be receiving these messages.

Nevertheless, there is one best practice that every successful e-mail campaign needs to employ: if you want a strong response from your e-mail campaign prospects, you first need to be relevant.

Let's get back to the realization that consumers are humans. In order for marketers' messages to communicate value, they first need to be perceived as personally meaningful by the recipient. As we talked about in earlier chapters, people are only going to pay attention to things that are personally important to them.

We all receive numerous e-mails per day, and yet most of us only open up a small percentage of those messages because we automatically filter them into groups of "important to me" and "not important to me" first. In truth, most everything we come into contact with on a daily basis goes through a similar process.

As consumers, we like things that make us feel comfortable. Comfort comes in many forms, and relevancy and familiarity are two of those. We generally determine relevancy by looking for cues that provide us with a deeper understanding of the meaning and value of an offer. For example, when we receive an e-mail in our inbox, we do a value assessment of that e-mail by looking for cues that communicate some sort of personal connection. For instance, we look for sender names we recognize, keywords that have meaning to us personally, relevant topics and themes that we consider personally meaningful, and messages from people we know or organizations we support.

Unfortunately, the average e-mail inbox looks like a high percentage of e-mail marketers don't really take into consideration the significant and personally relevant needs of consumers when they design their offers. Many offers seem to be, at best, an absolute shot in the dark when it comes to making a meaningful connection.

Because the cost of sending these e-mails was so insignificant, many advertisers focus more on reaching as many people as possible instead of on trying to reach the right people. Unfortunately, this approach also poisons the well by creating marketing noise that makes it more difficult for legitimate marketers to get the right message to the right consumer.

PLANNING AND DEVELOPMENT
STRATEGIES FOR E-MAIL CAMPAIGNS

At the core of everything we do as marketers is the desire to create a level of awareness and understanding.

Your customers understand that you're in business to make money. From them. However, there's a tactful way to approach people with whom you wish to do business so it doesn't feel like you're a predator looking for prey!

Like other types of marketing, e-mail marketing should be about finding ways to offer as much value as possible to your prospects and customers. This means making sure that every point of contact is not only relevant to those people but offers a reason to become and stay engaged.

E-mail campaigns represent a way to start a meaningful conversation with qualified recipients. After all, the goal isn't to send an e-mail but rather to send an e-mail to somebody who will care and respond in a meaningful way.

Marketers need to make an extra effort to treat the people they are contacting through their e-mail lists with the greatest respect. This includes not being condescending or treating people like they're all a soft touch. It also demands utmost honesty and transparency and a sense of credibility. Today's consumers not only know how to do their fact checking but also have their BS meters finely tuned to avoid anything that's too much like marketing speak. Marketers who lie or embellish the truth even a little can end up irreparably damaging their brands and looking unprofessional.

Finding commonality between an e-mail message and the needs and interests of target consumers is critical.

One way to achieve that commonality is to identify which holidays and personal events a consumer is likely to respond to. For many of us there are few things more personal to us than our birthdays, and e-mail messaging offers that cater to areas of self-interest generally catch our attention. The examples below represent a handful of potential approaches to make themselves uniquely relevant to the recipient. In other cases, sometimes it's the marketers themselves who have a special day they want to celebrate with recipients.

Figure 6.1   Event e-mail examples

Other special events can also create opportunities to make a meaningful connection with people. Taking advantage of holidays, significant special days on the calendar, seasonal changes, and even fun and made-up holidays (Talk Like a Pirate Day anyone?) are all great ways of creating points of commonality between a message and the needs and interests of the recipients.

Special events may also include weather events. While few advertisers are waiting for the next hurricane before they get their message out the door, some weather events, such as heat waves or cold snaps, can create an opportunity for marketers to find a point of commonality they can use to connect with prospects.

On the other hand, not all brands show sensitivity when dealing with human strife and suffering. For example, when Hurricane Sandy hit the US East Coast in 2012, a number of brands were able to share their understanding and empathy regarding the impact of the storm on many people in the greater New York area. Others, unfortunately, seem to have missed the emotional significance that this event had on many of their customers.

For example, Urban Outfitters set an e-mail out to their list a few days after the storm with the subject line "This storm blows (but guess what doesn't!)" during which the company offered a shopping promotion of 10 percent off plus free shipping to a local audience many of whom had no electricity for days or weeks following the storm. One of the most immediate outcomes of the campaign was that it quickly became viral among consumers who found the ad tacky and distasteful and started calling for boycotts.

Again, this brand had no malicious intent, but the company definitely came across to many as insensitive and opportunistic.

Another advertiser who ran afoul of this particular storm was Macy's. Macy's, like many stores, runs weekly sales offers. The e-mail that was sent out that particular week had a subject line promoting Macy's products at 20 percent off as part of its "hurricane relief pass," and the e-mail copy read "in the face of such massive hardship, we're here to lend you a helping hand." Again, if you're a consumer living through that sort of nightmare, this offer doesn't feel like humanitarian aid. It feels like an opportunistic attempt to link tragedy to a marketing program. As a mea culpa of sorts, Macy's followed this poorly timed campaign with a fund-raising message to help those most impacted by the storm.

INCREASING E-MAIL DELIVERABILITY RATES

A high percentage of e-mail deliverability is based on having accurate, permission-based addresses to work with.

This means that the e-mail addresses your companies uses are those of people who already know your brand or mission and have already expressed willingness to hear from you from time to time.

For marketers who rent e-mail lists there are deeper challenges. For starters, the people receiving e-mails from you in that case may not have any kind of relationship with your brands or mission. The people you want to contact are those who already understand the value proposition you offer. As a marketer, you will also want to be sure that the people you are reaching, whether through a homegrown or rental list, already have some sort of connection to your brand and understand what value you bring to the marketplace. The bottom line is that you want to talk to the right people who have the right intentions and not just to people who happen to be part of the database.

People like the sound of their own names. This means that marketers who use the names of their recipients as part of the subject line do a better job at grabbing attention and will increase e-mail open rates.

E-mail personalization requires a fair amount of planning to be successful. For starters, it means that marketers who want to send personalized messages first need to determine what types of personalized data they need to do the job. Then they need to find ways to collect that data. It's a fairly common practice these days to ask people submitting e-mail addresses to also share a preferred first name they use.

One other challenge with the personalization process is the need to fully understand the technology behind that process. All too often a broken personalization process sends the wrong overall message. As with everything else we do in digital media, we want to make sure that we test and retest everything before it goes out the door; otherwise a brand's credibility can be severely compromised if something goes wrong. Mistakes, such as sending a placeholder being sent in lieu of proper names, turn the personalization attempt into a bit of a joke and fail to impress.

HANDLING NEW E-MAIL SIGN-UPS

When people have given you permission to communicate with them in the future, treat this like the gift it is.

Greet them with open arms. Make them feel welcome, provide them with something of value and insights, and a little something to make them feel special. Offer them exclusive opportunities and share a little bit of love. We're serious about this. Make their permission an event to be celebrated. After all, without all these names and the real people at the other end of the channel who just gave you permission to contact them, you really have nothing. After all, the people we get to work with are the reason we are in business to begin with.

That said, it's not always easy, especially in smaller businesses, to greet each new arrival as a long-lost friend. That's where autoresponders come in.

Autoresponders offer online marketers the perfect blend of technology and strategy. An autoresponder, in the most basic terms, is an e-mail or a series of e-mails that are automatically sent to a new member of the e-mail database.

For example, a visitor to your website may decide that he or she wants to be part of your inner circle of information recipients and leaves a first name and e-mail address as part of the form you have on that page. After clicking the "submit" button to share that data, the first thing that happens is that the systems handling that data automatically sends an e-mail to the e-mail address submitted asking for further verification and rechecking that person's desire to be added to the e-mail database.

This e-mail generally contains a link the recipient must click on before the data is fully captured by the company. This double opt-in process (first opt-in when the "submit" button was clicked, the second when the link is clicked) covers several important bases. First of all, it verifies that the e-mail address being collected is legitimate and goes to an actual person. This way marketers can get an equitable trade for whatever benefits they are offering in exchange for the e-mail address.

Second, the second opt-in step prevents people from signing other people up for things they may not want. In the early days of e-mail it was possible (and not always an innocent prank) to sign other people up for all sorts of dubious and nuisance e-mail. Finally, and as we will explore later in this chapter, this step also helps marketers protect themselves from future complaints of spamming. The person who explicitly gives marketers permission for future contact generally isn't going to complain when e-mail starts showing up.

This process can also be extended to follow up with a "welcome" or "getting started" e-mail once the recipient has opted in twice. In this way the e-mail process can be automated and personalized and be able to reach out to new recipients 24/7.

The autoresponder process also allows marketers to create what is known as a messaging arc. A messaging arc is basically a preselected list of e-mails and a schedule for their delivery.

Let's say that you are collecting e-mail addresses for the purposes of lead generation. The people who are signing up are expressing some interest in your products and services but are not yet ready to make a purchase. They need more information, a greater understanding of the value and benefits, some time to share the news with other people in their lives, etc. What a messaging arc can do is to provide a prescheduled list of follow-up e-mails that can be sent in the hours or days following the prospect's initial sign-up.

For example, a welcome e-mail could be scheduled as a follow-up almost immediately upon receiving the double opt-in confirmation. A messaging arc could then be put into place that has rules determining, for instance, that five days after the welcome e-mail goes out, please follow up with a second e-mail that speaks a little bit more about the value of the products and services being offered. A third e-mail could then be scheduled as a follow-up two weeks after that to provide a little bit more information or a link to a video that shows the product in action. This process allows marketers to follow up in a timely manner without having to also manage the entire process outside of getting the e-mails created and set up in the first place.

A messaging arc can take on the role of both sales and marketing teams by offering periodic follow-ups and can be used to drive prospects further into the sales funnel by giving them the insights and understanding they need to make an informed buying decision.

BUILDING THE PERFECT E-MAIL

The biggest obstacle that all e-mail marketers face is that of getting their messages noticed and then opened.

The following best practices strategies can make all the difference between sending e-mail that blends in with the crowd and e-mail that gets noticed and opened by the people you most want to reach.

The Importance of the Recognizable Sender

The name used in a received e-mail helps to answer the consumer's main question: "Who wants my attention and why?"

One of the easiest ways to get positive results from an e-mail campaign is to make sure that the sender name is meaningful to the e-mail recipient. As we mentioned before, most people scan their incoming e-mail looking for something familiar or relevant to them. This includes names they recognize. These can be the names of friends, brands, and businesses or even the names of celebrities and spokespeople for different organizations. However, the names we use in our e-mail campaigns are an important jumping-off point. Names represent a "face" for a brand or service.

When sending out e-mails it's important that marketers consider the value of making a personal connection by using a consistent brand tag or sender name. While the recipients may have no idea who Bob Smith is the first few times they receive an e-mail from an organization or a brand, over time the relationship between Bob Smith and that brand will start to become clear. This doesn't necessarily mean that there's a relevancy between that message and the recipient, but it does mean that the recipients will start to recognize Bob's name and that will change the overall value perception of the message in their minds.

The Craft of Meaningful Subject Lines

While the sender name used when sending e-mail is important, perhaps there's nothing more important to gain the attention of a recipient than the e-mail's subject line. So what is the best subject line to use to get the desired results?

Because every e-mail campaign is completely different and for a different target audience and different campaign objectives, there is no single subject line messaging solution to be offered. However, there are some best practices to keep in mind.

A study done by the e-mailing company MailChimp in 2013 found that e-mails bearing subject lines of 50 characters or less often had greater open rates. This is attributed to additional white space that can catch attention in a sea of text. The one caveat to this is when sending e-mails to a list of people who know you well and will appreciate the additional information in the subject line.

So which is it, longer subject lines or shorter subject lines? The answer, as for most things in marketing, is "it depends."

For e-mail to make a personal connection with the recipient it has to offer some points of relevancy and significance. This includes meaningful keywords included in the subject line, clear value propositions, information that meshes well with the needs of a recipient, and meaningful personalization.

We like to think of an e-mail's subject line as the place where marketers can start telling a compelling story. This includes using relevant names and words as part of their presentation. It also means finding a way to answer the recipients' question of why they should care. In addition, the subject line should highlight special features that may be included as part of the e-mail experience, such as promoting videos, news updates, special events, and special offers.

The average person receiving an email is looking for some relevant value or personal benefit. Be certain to include this information in your subject line if appropriate. In certain cases, an injection of humor or a promise of intrigue and interest as part of the e-mail subject line (and this should always be done tastefully) can also be a key to getting e-mails seen and opened. The message that this content is interesting and well worth the recipients' time to check it out can make a huge difference in overall open rates.

In addition, you should include keywords that resonate with recipients to get them to pay attention to the e-mail. These may include industry acronyms, jargon, and other items that may be best understood by people who can best take advantage of an offer in a particular industry.

Creating Impactful E-mail Messages

One of the decisions you will need to make before you send out an e-mail campaign is whether or not your recipients would rather have text-based e-mails or HTML-based e-mails. Currently, most e-mail clients have no problem dealing with HTML-based e-mails; however, some folks still prefer to have graphics turned off in order to speed up the e-mail and to forestall viruses and other security issues. The main advantage of text-based e-mails is that they pretty much can be received by anybody receiving e-mail regardless of the e-mail client used. Because HTML e-mails are more complex and often rely on attachments of graphics and other media, there are more things that can go wrong.

On the other hand, one of the main advantages of HTML content is that the messages are generally more attractive and eye-catching. The use of graphics and other multimedia assets makes the messages look better and more user-friendly. Of course, a link to a video can also be placed in a text-based e-mail, but overall that format just isn't as visually appealing.

One way to better determine which format you should use for outgoing e-mail campaigns is to ask your recipients when they opt in to your list which they prefer. Then it's a simple matter of creating two separate lists, each catering to a separate audience. This way you can make sure that the format recipients desire is the one they receive.

Keep It Simple, Stupid

There are a number of different schools of thought with regard to how much content should be included in a single e-mail message. There are plenty of old-school marketers who get great results from incredibly long messages that continuously introduce and reinforce key buying points for their products and services.

On the other hand, there are plenty of marketers who want to cut to the chase as quickly as possible to make sure that they are able to communicate what they need in the limited time of engagement they have when the recipient opens an e-mail.

We're both big fans of less content saying more. Less content also creates an opportunity to follow up in the future with additional e-mails that offer ever greater insight into an offer.

It's also realistic to assume that most people really don't want to make the time or have the inclination to read a lot of text. They want to know what the benefits are as quickly as possible so they can make a decision or move on. By focusing on the main message and providing recipients with a strong call to action, savvy marketers are able to capture more interest and allow the recipients to process benefits and values more quickly.

It has been our experience that if prospects feel like they're receiving too much information at once, they may just avoid the message entirely. This means that you should quickly communicate how easy it is to get to the good stuff and benefits being offered. We're both big fans of using video clips for these purposes. Video represents an easy and convenient way to move a lot of information in the shortest period of time. Videos are generally engaging as well as easy to assimilate.

There is also an additional added value when using video because it is possible to measure the overall impact and overall engagement of the e-mail by measuring the average length of time that a recipient spends watching a video. For example, a 30-second video that measures that 83 percent of people who click on its link watch the entire clip tells a very different story from a similar video that shows that only 17 percent of people who click on its link watched it all the way to the end. While this news might not make marketers happy, this type of feedback loop is a fantastic indicator of which content best resonates and engages recipients and offers a golden opportunity to make improvements in this area.

Working with E-mail Lists and List Brokers

When it comes to e-mail addresses, there are really three ways that marketers can acquire e-mail lists:

1. Steal e-mail addresses by randomly surfing the web in search of the @ symbol. Sell those e-mail addresses to legitimate marketers who think they're getting a good deal but who are actually setting themselves up for a world of spam-related hurt or use them yourself to create special offers that have subject lines like "D.i.s.c.o.u.n.t. V1agra!" This approach works best if you have no moral compass and don't mind being a complete dirtbag. Wait, on second thought, don't ever do this!

2. Rent e-mail address lists. While renting lists can be a very quick way of reaching a target audience, using rented lists is also fraught

with potential challenges and some serious pitfalls. For starters, most of the people you will reach through any list that you rent are not people who opted in to receive e-mail messages from you. As a result, recipients may complain about you sending unsolicited e-mails to them and can even lead to your legitimate marketing efforts being blacklisted as spam in some cases.

The other main challenge of rental lists, apart from the varying price values, is that sometimes the lists you rent are poorly managed, contain many dead or out-of-date addresses, contain duplicated addresses, and may be of dubious origin. Keep in mind that what really works here is to create a personal relationship with everybody you need to talk to and that leads us to the next point.

3. Create your own list. Creating your own mailing list is a slow and very organic process. It's also a much more meaningful way to communicate with people who want to hear from you (or at least won't be offended if you contact them) since they've already gone through a double opt-in process (they have, haven't they?)

Creating your own list means, first, creating a way to collect e-mail addresses. In most cases this is done by creating sections of web sites and landing pages that share with visitors the benefits they will receive in exchange for sharing their personal information. Keep in mind that the quality of an e-mail list is directly related to the reason those people joined this list. For example, if the reason people are willing to share their e-mail address is for a sweepstake or some sort of prize giveaway, then marketers may be able to generate a lot of interest and collect a lot of e-mail addresses, but it may also be difficult to engage with the list of people in the future if there isn't another equally big offer or opportunity. For marketers who offer something of value and meaning to a predetermined audience, such as a white paper or a download of a study or sample or access to an informative video, the response rates will generally be much lower but the resulting list will consist of self-qualified prospects who have a high chance of being genuinely interested in an offer related to your goods and services.

Practical Wisdom—In e-mail marketing, as in other areas of the digital realm, the impact of GIGO (garbage in, garbage out) can be significant. While a rented list may be aboveboard in terms of how the data was collected, it's always a good idea to get as much of a list "pedigree" as possible. A number of list brokers compile e-mail lists by offering online contests or giveaways. While there's nothing inherently wrong with this approach, consumers who are willing to give up their e-mail address because they want to win something are very different from those who share their data because they want to be included in future communications with an advertiser. When possible, focus on creating lists that are based on genuine interest and cater to specific consumer needs and don't just belong to a warm body who really wants to win a sports car.

This means that you need to make sure that every point of contact you have with your prospects should be relevant to them and their needs. It also means that future contact with these people can't be about your brand or your offer first and foremost but should focus on their needs and how you can help them meet their needs.

In a lot of ways e-mail marketing is a form of no-sales selling. It's about providing opportunities for consumers to get involved with a brand or an offer but doing so in such a subtle way that it feels very low pressure and beneficial to consumers.

This includes not being condescending or treating people like they may not know what's going on. It also demands utmost honesty. We live in a world where the average consumer has the ability to check facts in mere seconds. Marketers who embellish the truth or even tell white lies to consumers can quickly lose credibility.

The bottom line is that you want to offer value to your e-mail recipients every time and make sure that everything you do not only in your e-mail marketing but in every facet of your online and off-line marketing is aboveboard. It really is that easy.

E-MAIL LIST MANAGEMENT STRATEGIES

As you create your own in-house list, you will find a need to break that list into smaller segments.

These segments will represent different types of customers and prospects based on their needs along with where they might be within your sales funnel. For starters, it's very probable that you'll want to have slightly different conversations with different groups of people on your list. For example, a prospect who becomes a customer is not only going to have different level of understanding regarding the value and benefits of the brands and services your company offers but is also in a very different place from someone who has never become a customer. As a result, marketers want to create messages that specifically promote what those prospects would want by focusing more on reasons why these prospects should become customers. Other segments of the e-mail list may focus more on messages that promote repurchasing or even on upselling opportunities.

Practical Wisdom—While we're both huge fans of keeping databases of consumer personalization information, ordering history, and other personal preferences, sometimes data personalization can backfire. For example, a few years ago a friend placed an order with the national online florist to send his mother a Mother's Day bouquet. Sadly, during the following year his mother passed away. The next year, as Mother's Day approached, this company dutifully sent out a reminder to him to make sure he got his Mother's Day flower order in early so that he could surprise his mom. While certainly the intent of the message was not malicious, it ended up being a sad reminder of loss and not one of celebration.

More recently an office supply company direct mail piece went viral after the recipient posted it online. On the envelope that arrived were the addressee's name and street address and a separate line that read, "Daughter killed in car crash." Yes, it happened, and sadly the mailer arrived almost a year to the day after the young woman and her boyfriend were tragically killed in a car accident. You can only imagine how well this was received.

As marketers we can easily understand that at some point data was mined from local media and added to this man's contact information by the store. What we can't imagine is how or when this kind of information would come in handy for a company selling office supplies. Is there an ongoing bereavement special? Is the store planning on creating a scholarship in the girl's name? Our takeaway is that this kind of data, while accurate, is virtually useless. Don't collect it if you can't use it.

It's worth mentioning that when collecting personally identifiable information (PII) from consumers, marketers need to carefully think about what data they want to capture and why.

For example, most consumers consider it a fair exchange to give a name and e-mail address if they're going able to get something of value in return. Most reason that the worst thing that can happen to them if they share e-mail data is that they will receive an e-mail from that marketer in the future. But when marketers start asking for other types of data, especially home addresses and phone numbers, most consumers will start to feel that the exchange is no longer equitable. There's a big difference between sharing an e-mail address and telling marketers where you live and giving them access to your phone 24/7. In short, for many consumers this type of interaction goes from being a simple exchange of information and starts to feel more like an invasion of privacy. As a result, a campaign trying to collect this data will see significantly fewer people willing to do so.

The bottom line is that if you don't have an explicit reason for collecting data, then don't. Less is more from a marketing standpoint. It also means less chance of future liability, and you can better defend your privacy stance when you have less consumer data to protect.

The same holds true for messages going out to prospects who are new to an e-mail database and for people who have been long-time prospects but have never made a purchase or a list of people who are repeat or frequent customers. Each one of these lists is going to need to have a unique message that focuses more on their existing relationship with your brand and how you would like to leverage that relationship in the future.

You're going to work hard to get people to join your e-mail list. The ultimate goal is to keep as many qualified people on that list as possible. It may also mean culling out those people who never open messages, never respond, and really don't bring any value to the table.

List management success also means that you are able to consistently provide list members with messages that are relevant and also give them something of value each time. The challenge here is that this value is based entirely upon the recipient's perspective. As savvy marketers, we try to make every message count as something new or unique but the biggest challenge is that for many of the people we reach receiving too many e-mails from the same marketers can lead to brand and list burnout. This often makes people who have been good prospects opt out of lists because they are feeling overwhelmed with content.

So how do you determine the best level of frequency for sending out e-mails to your list? The best approach is to ask your list members about their preferences when you are collecting their e-mail data in the first place.

Asking prospects when they sign up to join a mailing list how frequently they would like to receive updates from your company and brand is a fantastic best practice. While it does mean that you will need to further segment your lists, it also allows you to do a better job of meeting the expectations and needs of prospects while creating a multitiered approach for how you communicate with these people.

UNDERSTANDING E-MAIL CAMPAIGN
CAN-SPAM COMPLIANCE

Here's an interesting challenge: if you were to ask average people on the street to define what e-mail spam is what would they tell you? In our experience, the general answer most often boils down to something like "spam is e-mail sent to me that I don't want."

The reality of spam, at least in legal terms, is that just because a message is unsolicited, it is not necessarily spam. We all get plenty of e-mail daily that we didn't ask for and may not want, but the majority of it can't be classified as spam in legal terms.

In some cases spam is poorly defined as e-mail that has been sent in bulk. But once again there are plenty of legitimate marketers who send out hundreds of thousands of e-mails at one time to well-developed lists and are fully compliant with CAN-SPAM laws.

CAN-SPAM stands for: Controlling the Assault of Non-Solicited Pornography And Marketing Act of 2003. And while this legislation was a welcome attempt to regulate the volume of fraudulent and offensive e-mails being sent, in reality it's done very little to stem the tide of questionable and vastly irrelevant offers most of use receive daily.

To make things more confusing, the guidelines for what is considered spam and what isn't are still often open to interpretation. However, for an e-mail to be considered CAN-SPAM compliant it needs to effectively address three different areas of compliance:

unsubscribe compliance
content compliance
sending behavior compliance

Unsubscribe compliance refers to the inclusion of a visible and operable unsubscribe mechanism in all e-mails. If you look through the list of e-mails you receive on a daily basis in most cases if you scroll to the bottom of those messages, you will find a link that will allow you to opt out of that mailing list. Unsubscribe compliance also requires that any consumer opt-out requests are honored within 10 business days. For many legitimate marketers the opt-out process is handled almost immediately after a request.

Content compliance offers guidelines for what is acceptable and allowed as part of an e-mail message and, among other things, requires that the sender addresses are accurate. The same provision also requires that subject lines be relevant to the content recipients will find when they open the e-mail (and not a matter of bait and switch), and the body content of the e-mail must be free from banned images, links, and other legally governed content.

Content compliance also requires that marketers include a legitimate physical address, either their own or that of an advertiser they represent, in the footer of the e-mail. This ruling is designed to create a higher level of transparency based on the assumption that legitimate marketers would have no reason or need to hide their location or place of business from the world.

Finally, sending behavior compliance has more to do with the technology being used to send a message to a list. This includes not sending e-mails through servers that use an open mail relay, which offers few guidelines for protections against spamming or anonymous use by others. Send behavior compliance also covers never using a harvested e-mail list. A harvested e-mail list is a list that many spammers use that is created by using robot programs that search the web looking for the @ symbol as a way of determining potential e-mail addresses. These addresses are generally the fodder for spam campaigns.

Legitimate marketers need to be aware of these guidelines and include them as part of their marketing best practices. However, one challenge that remains is that spam is often in the eye of the beholder or in this case the recipient. Even legitimate marketers who follow the guidelines can sometimes run afoul of a recipient's tolerance and understanding of what spam is, and their messages may be placed on an e-mail blacklist if an ISP gets too many complaints.

The challenge is that it's very hard to get off a blacklist without jumping through a number of legal hoops. Again, many of the third-party companies that marketers can work with for e-mail campaigns will also monitor events in which a marketer's e-mail address has been flagged as belonging to a spammer. Being forewarned of trouble can mean being able to resolve an issue before it really becomes a problem.

CAN-SPAM COMPLIANCE STRATEGIES FOR E-MAIL CAMPAIGN

Getting an e-mail message to a recipient is far from being a slam dunk even if you have the cleanest and best managed list in the world.

The following best practices can make a huge difference in the overall success of an e-mail campaign:

Avoid Using Large Graphics or Fully Graphical E-mail Content

Throughout the years the practice of single graphic e-mails has often been associated with spam. As a result, high-level spam filters may be looking for any e-mails that have a large ratio of graphics, especially single graphics that make up the entire body of the message. Apart from taking up a much larger data footprint than text messages, these messages rate high on the spam scan. Once again, it doesn't matter if a marketer's intention is to spam or not. If a message is perceived as spam, then the odds of it being delivered a reduced dramatically.

Do Not Send Bulk E-mail from Your Personal or Business E-mail Account

Once again, many Internet service providers try to minimize spam coming from their servers by looking for "bad guys" who are sending bulk e-mail messages. What constitutes bulk e-mail? It's a great question that has many different answers. Bulk e-mail may be considered by some servers as few as 50 e-mails being sent out at one time. We've all heard stories about brides-to-be who found their personal email accounts blocked because they had the audacity to send out several hundred emails at once to friends and family. It's probably safe to say that these messages are generally not CAN-SPAM compliant either! However, common sense also makes it pretty obvious that this type of behavior is not the work of a spammer. That said, once an e-mail account has been blacklisted, it's not an easy process to convince an ISP that your intentions were noble.

While renting or buying e-mail lists is certainly not illegal, we encourage you to use extreme caution when using e-mail lists that are your own to reach prospects and customers. Once again, spam is in the eye of the beholder, and recipients receiving a message from your company may take steps to report you as a spammer because they didn't give you direct permission to contact them. While this may be an overreaction, a small percentage of people are actively trying to rid the world of spammers one e-mail at a time.

WORKING WITH THIRD-PARTY E-MAIL SERVICE PROVIDERS

We encourage our clients to work with third-party e-mail sending and monitoring companies whenever possible. Not only can these companies help protect your brands and corporate communication from spam and other abuses but they can also track campaign specifics, such as the deliverability of e-mail and other response metrics.

These reports also provide marketers with rich insights into campaign effectiveness and allow them to measure the deliverability rate of an e-mail (including soft and hard bounces), the click through rate, unique clicks, and whether specific links were followed.

Many of these systems are also able to automatically segment e-mail lists based on consumer behaviors (such as who did or didn't open an e-mail or if people opened it what level of interaction followed).

This means that marketers can approach prospects who never open or respond in any way to newsletters or other e-mail announcements differently from those who occasionally view incoming e-mails. Creating this list gives marketers the opportunity to create separate campaigns that focus more on trying to engage with prospects by identifying more meaningful conversation starting points.

For example, those prospects that opened an e-mail but didn't click on any links might receive a follow-up e-mail that encourages them to drill a little deeper to learn more about the benefits and value of an offer. Those recipients who didn't even open the e-mail may receive a message that encourages them to start by opening the e-mail so that they can learn more about the benefits. An additional e-mail could be created for prospects who occasionally read the e-mails and click on links. Overall, this approach helps marketers step away from "one-size-fits-all" models and do a more effective job of addressing the specific needs and interests of the different individuals and segments that can make up a list.

CHAPTER 7

SEARCH ENGINE ADVERTISING

Searching and finding should be the simplest thing the connected digital marketing world has to offer.

You can't imagine the joy a search can represent. Enter a word in the box, and the most relevant information the world has to offer is returned to you, gift-wrapped with an endorsement from people just like you. At its core, search marketing isn't any more complicated than a simple equation: declared intent + information consumption options = efficient Internet.

In its purest form during the early days of development, search had no advertisements or commercial value to speak of; it was just a way for people to find information they wanted. It was the yellow pages with no ads. In fact, the early ads in search were very close cousins to the ads we've been seeing in phone books for over a century. Display ads that were triggered by keyword searches were the early standard of online advertising. Search sites weren't "engines" but "directories," compiled and managed by human beings. However, when the mass of information on the web began exceed the human capacity to index it, some guys figured out how to use math and automated software to do the job with fewer people involved. Google was born, and the rest is history.

In the next two chapters we'll talk about the art of connecting intent with marketing.

SEARCH MARKETING FUNDAMENTALS

The search engine began with one simple goal: help organize what we used to refer to as the World Wide Web's information.

It's only fitting that we begin with a public service announcement: we'd like to clarify one very important truth in the business of search marketing. The phrase "search engine marketing" refers to the combined disciplines of paid advertising (sponsored links, ads, and their ilk) and search engine optimization (anything in search that isn't available on a cost-per-click basis.) People refer to SEM as the paid side and to SEO as the natural side, but in reality they are two sides of the same coin.

Let's take a quick look at the search marketing landscape and clarify some basic concepts.

The Basics

Search is simple, right?

Type a question in the form of a keyword into a search box and get the answer you need.

Well, here's where it gets more complicated: people are inconsistent.

You don't build websites or products for robots; you build them for people. And when you introduce the needs, demands, and expectations of people, everything gets a whole lot more complicated.

Search is intent-based marketing. A search query is an expression of that intent. Over the years, much has been written about the advancement of declared intent.

Anybody can look at a keyword and make a connection to what the searcher is looking for, right?

Well, yes, to a certain extent.

But there is an art to search marketing—a knack for looking beyond the obvious to uncover the underlying motivation driving the searcher to seek this particular information.

Tap this insight to connect searchers to (your) meaningful content, and you will see your business grow despite the vast competition you face or the depth of their pockets.

As with any other form of marketing, mastering the art of search starts with knowing your customers.

The industry can evolve, technology can proliferate, and keywords can all but disappear, but if the customer is at the center or your search strategy, you will prevail.

The Fundamentals of Search Marketing

Search marketing breaks down into two main disciplines: paid search advertising (which we'll get right into) and organic search optimization (which we'll get into in our next chapter.)

Paid search advertising (aka paid search, SEM, PPC, or sponsored search) is the act of bidding in a keyword auction for your text ad to appear within a designated section of the search engine results page (SERP) when someone you have targeted performs a search you deem relevant to your business.

Paid search advertising is bought on a per-click basis rather than an impression model. Bids are placed in real-time. There is no discount, up-front inventory, or make good. You bid on a keyword and are charged when someone clicks through to your website.

Search Marketing Strategy 1: We Can't All Build Hotels on Broadway and Park Place

A smart search strategy should start with a wish list of keyword categories you want coverage for followed by a competitive analysis to understand what it would cost for you to own any sort of consistent share of voice (SOV) in those categories.

Just as with anything else, you start with your wish list and you compromise.

That's where "integration" comes in. Yes, the word has been overused to the point of having no meaning. But what it actually *means* when we talk search strategy is balancing media investment with content optimization/ investment to round out your coverage of SERP real estate.

If you have identified a high-value segment of keywords that you cannot support with media, you now know that you have to invest in more content development and outreach to build your organic authority for these keywords; we'll say more about that later.

As a best practice, every piece of content you put online should be targeting a specific keyword that you have identified as having high value. This is true for both paid and organic SEO.

When you approach customers, do you ramble on incessantly about every single thing you do when they ask you for information on one specific product or service? We hope not. So why would you do that when communicating with them online? As we've mentioned several times so far in this book, your success starts with keeping your end goal in mind when you begin any campaign.

Build content that answers the questions customers have about your product or service. Everything you communicate should be for the benefit of your target audience. Avoid creating campaigns designed to impress the company's board of directors unless the directors are your target audience.

Search Marketing Strategy 2: Learn the Tools of the Trade

Select your tools the same way a chef selects his ingredients. Too much of any one ingredient can spoil the finished product. The simple fact that there are so many tools available combined with the volatile nature of technology funding means a lot of coming and going for software or tool companies.

As a general rule, we advise against the all-in-one tool for the same reason we recommend storing eggs in multiple baskets. Likewise, any list of the top tools has a shelf life about five hours in today's digital marketing ecosystem. These lists are a relatively large waste of time.

It's also a very good idea to look at "top <insert any product>" lists and "reports" with a skeptical eye. Many of these look like third-party ratings, but in reality they are nothing more than well-funded advertising or public relations placements for these companies. Similarly, steer clear of downloadable free (only if you surrender your e-mail address and opt-in for a barrage of sales pitches) reports.

To illustrate the point of how short the shelf life for any tool can be in a rapidly changing technological environment, figure 7.1 depicts a group

Company Focus Evolution

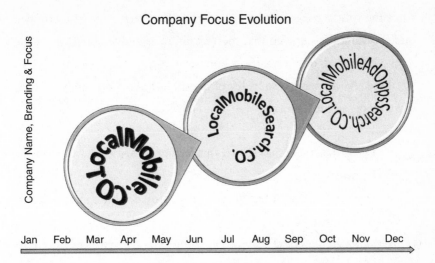

Figure 7.1   Company focus evolution

of major players in the search marketing arena less than a year ago. Today, through mergers and acquisitions, branding changes and good old-fashioned attrition, many of these brands no longer exist. This isn't to say that there's anything wrong with any of the companies depicted, just that the environment is constantly changing. In short, focus more on your needs as a marketer and not on the lists of possible solutions when getting started.

It's also important to note that many of the tools offered in the paid search realm are being offered by the same people selling you ads. Search engines offer many of the best tools in the business. Just remember that these tools function in the matter best befitting the search engine's needs. They are also easy to use, intuitive, and fast. However, the need for a third-party perspective is essential when buying media. Furthermore, as we covered in the analytics chapter, the ability to compare analytics across multiple formats and media providers on your own terms is an important component of any online advertising initiative.

As the demand for more sophisticated tools increases and as the software costs decrease, the level of sophisticated information at your fingertips will increase exponentially. Unfortunately, you still have to try to understand it all. For the modern marketer even cheap software solutions can be expensive in terms of a significant commitment of resources. In the search engine advertising world, recommendations are cheap; your ability to define your strategy will be the difference between having an effective and measurable campaign that meets your goals and simply helping the sales rep meet his or her quarterly bonus.

Let's take a look at a short list of questions to help dig into your paid search tool selection process:

- Does the potential search marketing provider have industry knowledge?
- Does the potential search marketing provider have knowledge of your industry?
- Does the potential search marketing provider have the ability to offer you a managed services option?
- Does the potential search marketing provider offer multilingual support?
- Does the potential search marketing provider have the ability to illustrate tactical capabilities and efficient, flexible processes?

Industry knowledge might seem obvious, but in reality the people building software or offering software as a service might know less about the services they are offering than about how to build software.

Knowledge of your industry is also key. If you're in the retail category, it's not going to make a whole lot of sense for you to be looking at something in the manufacturing management area. Managed services are relatively new for software providers. Basically, you'll be able to get access to some of the services that you would normally see from a professional services company or agency.

Not having unlimited funds, many advertisers have turned to tools that enable spending efficiencies across multiple ad formats and media providers. Quite a few top-tier advertisers have built their own tools. These tools give you an important third-party perspective on spending and function by sending your campaign data to search sites.

When digging into tools, advertisers must remember to complete a comprehensive needs analysis prior to selecting any technology solution. In other words, a deep understanding of your problems before expecting software to fix them will go a long way toward ensuring that your resources are allocated efficiently.

Here's a short list of must-haves for software partners:

1. Seek out peer input
2. Look for proof of concept
3. Identify your exact need
4. Clearly define contract length and billing terms
5. Ensure current and future compatibility with existing tools

It may seem obvious to seek out peer input, but you'd be surprised how many people don't do it. Often the perspectives and insights you need to better understand an approach or strategy is as near as the person in the next cubicle or across the hall. There are lots of technologies out there, and what we mean by proof of concept is that the solutions you're considering should have been tried and tested beyond canned endorsements. There is absolutely nothing wrong with asking to speak with a vendor's live client as part of doing your due diligence.

The bottom line is that you want to make sure that your essential needs as a marketer are being addressed by any solution you adopt. Remember: everything is negotiable. An overabundance of competition in this arena has driven down costs, and anything on the table is open to customization based on your brand's unique needs. You name it—contract length, billing terms, free trial periods, custom demos with your data, and managed services versus self-service—all these are options.

PAID SEARCH" AD CREATION

In search, successful marketers dedicate countless hours to the hunt for the perfect keywords.

Over the years, we've seen just about every form of keyword development—brainstorming sessions, dedicated teams, specialized software, data mining, to name a few. Meanwhile, many of the resulting ads appear to have been written without much thought.

Many search marketers end up obsessing about their campaign's quality score. Depending on who you ask, quality score is either a solid way to ensure an efficient user experience or a really effective way for Google to consistently increase its revenues.

Ad copy for paid search ads is undoubtedly the stepchild of SEM, and many marketers are paying for their lack of stewardship in this area. The wayward nature of poor copy is a product of the quantitative nature of search and indeed performance marketing in general. Numbers and creative are not good bedfellows.

Better ranking for paid search ads on Google is all about quality score, and quality score is all about relevance and click-through rate (CTR). If marketers wish to improve their quality score for their ads and thus increase their rankings and lower their click costs, they need to focus on their ad copy with the same intensity they show in discovering the keywords that make up their campaigns.

How does all this come together in one perfect, little package? Let's take a look.

The Perfect Search

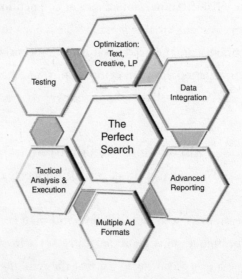

Figure 7.2 The perfect search

AVOID USING KEYWORD INSERTION AS A STRATEGY

We've all seen this before: the paid search ad that shows up during a routine hunt for information and just doesn't make any sense. We're not talking about poorly written copy either but about an ad that just baffles the imagination with its complete lack of logic or meaning. These ads were probably the result of keyword insertion (see figure 7.2).

When search ads first started to appear on the scene, advertisers ended up using keywords from search queries to create ads on the fly. The results were often cringeworthy as companies presented ads helping consumers to find deals on "terrorists." "genocide," and in the case of a celebrity whose child had just died, it even offered "a new child." But it gets worse.

Humans and Search Advertising

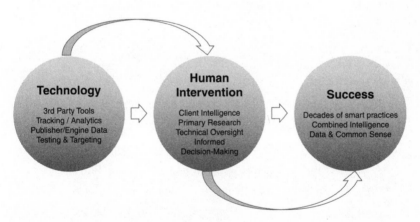

Figure 7.3   Humans and search engine advertising

Practical Wisdom—Not long after performing an audit or opportunity analysis on a company that had been running ads on keywords for every category under the sun with most of the terms set to be a broad match and almost all of the ads utilizing KWI to cover a lack of creativity and effort, a report came in from an angry customer who had witnessed an ad similar to this one:

Looking for Heroin?
Find it at XXXXX.com!

Apparently the company was buying terms associated with methadone clinics on a broad match, and Google made the leap. Throw in a little KWI and suddenly your company looks like it's selling smack. We imagine that ad had to be losing thousands of dollars a week just from the curious searchers out there clicking on the ad just to see what was on the other side.

The fun doesn't stop there. I'm sure just about everybody has caught one version of an ad generated by a major retailer using KWI to create the ads. Prospects searching for the word "stupid" or "crazy" or some other similarly unflattering term were seeing ads along the lines of:

Looking for Stupid?
Find Stupid in your size
At XXXX today!

Those are just the crazy examples, but there are plenty more that are less crazy but just as lazy and damaging to your campaign.

The lesson learned here is that you need to take the time to write individually targeted ads that line up nicely with the keywords you're utilizing in a given ad group lest your copy be incongruent and misused. Remember that paid search ad campaigns are the public face of your company, and a poorly written one will turn off a customer faster than a bad rating from the health department.

Just as with your driver's license or spandex pants, keyword insertion (KWI) is a privilege, not a right. If you're going to use this powerful tool in your campaign, you need to use it sparingly and as part of a rotation of other ads. Ad optimization means you should never be running just one ad creative in an ad group no matter how effective you think it will be. There is real safety in numbers here. Create many different ads and then let the market decide which ones are getting the job done.

While you're at it, try to avoid using KWI in ad groups that are heavily filled with broad match terms, lest you end up enthusiastically advertising something you don't even sell in the best of circumstances or don't want to get arrested for in the worst of circumstances. Remember, when you use broad match, Google will make the leap to other keywords you didn't even think of when creating your campaign, so be careful about using negative terms to keep out the riffraff and write your ad creative with the possibility that something strange my arise from an odd keyword insertion.

OPTIMIZATION: ARE YOU DOING IT RIGHT?

Paid search success often requires peeking into the various nooks and crannies of a market over time.

During the opportunity analysis process for paid search, we discover all kinds of weird things during audits. We tell our clients that if we don't find anything wrong with a paid search campaign during an audit, then we will offer that audit for free. We feel safe making this offer because we always find something wrong during an audit, and that something is usually hidden somewhere in the ad creative.

There are a lot of moving parts in a paid search campaign, especially with large-scale campaigns that are spread out across multiple accounts with millions of keywords and hundreds of different combinations of ad creative. After looking out across the sea of possible actions to take with the behemoth that is your Google account, you may feel lost and confused about where to start. Here's some advice on one of the first things you can do to juice up your campaigns to the next level: Go in right now and look at that rat's nest you call your creative strategy and straighten that thing out.

For starters, remind yourself of what it is you're actually trying to accomplish with your paid search campaign. Is it just traffic? No, it's probably something much more complex, such as new leads or sales or downloads or free trials or whatever. Basically, you are aiming for some way of converting a visitor into a customer so that your company makes money. Now ask yourself if your goal lies at the end of a sales funnel, why are you automatically optimizing your ads based on CTR?

Until just recently, Google's ad rotation settings had two options: rotate or optimize for clicks. In the first quarter of 2011, Google added in option of optimizing for conversions if your campaign was tied into conversion tracking or Google Analytics. However, before that time, you were probably basing your entire creative optimization strategy on some faith-based initiative (praying for good campaign results) rather than on the cold, hard numbers that actually confirm that either creative A or B are meeting your goal. Even if you took the extra step of tracking conversions by way of URL or some other form of tracking, there's a really good chance you were still goofing up enough that you ditched a perfectly good piece of creative because its CTR or conversion rate was lower than that of another piece of creative.

We know that nine times out of ten clients do not collect enough data to establish statistical significance—that is, to apply the formulaic approach for determining whether enough data was collected to provide enough confidence that one decision is better than another. Most of the time, when we ask how the winner was determined between a new piece of creative and an older, trusted piece of creative, we hear, "Oh, we just gave it a couple of weeks and made a gut call based on the CTR." Congratulations, we hope you and your gut are very happy together when you have to explain to your boss why you're losing money on a campaign that is getting lots of clicks but not making any money.

For those of you who don't want to trust this decision making to fate, there are formulas to use. Sure, these are complex formulas that make you use a part of your brain that has been long dormant since grad school, but formulas just the same. Luckily, there are a few smart folks who have developed web tools or downloadable Excel spreadsheets that will do the heavy lifting for you now. A typical spreadsheet will allow you to enter the impressions and clicks or the clicks and CTR for the control and the variation, and the formula will show whether you gathered enough data for the test to be considered significant. After you determine the winner, go back in there and write another variant. Like Sisyphus' task, your work will never be done here.

PAID SEARCH: MOBILE

In the past year or so, mobile search ad formats have arrived. Soothsayers have been saying "this is the year mobile will arrive" for the better part of a decade. This is how we know mobile has arrived: costs per <insert price metric> have increased exponentially in the past year or so.

Much as folks tend to group all aspects of text listings together because it's easier, advertisers have a tendency to test the waters of mobile without really investing in it. Without rewriting the mobile search advertising guide, here are a couple of things to take with you.

- There are fewer ads running on mobile channels so competition will raise prices quickly and unpredictably.
- Test and think about your landing pages. Since many people are just making a call, you may not even want landing pages.
- As we will explore further in chapter 10, mobile channels offer their own unique opportunities and challenges to marketers. For search marketing here are a few strategies you should be aware of.

Understanding Search Default Settings

Now that you're dying to know more about this hidden money waster buried within the depths of Google AdWords, head over to the "Networks and devices" area under the "Settings" tab and focus more on devices than networks. There you'll see two radio buttons that read, "All available devices (Recommended for new advertisers)" and "Let me choose...." That is a pretty heavy-handed "recommended" given that it's the default setting for all new campaigns. That's right, you've been advertising on devices in addition to people's desktops and laptops for all this time without really noticing. You've also been advertising on mobile devices, including Androids, Blackberries, iPhones, iPads, and just about every other phone with a screen, no matter how your site looks when it shows up on your mother's Razr phone from the beginning of the decade.

In case you were wondering, Search engies don't give away the clicks on mobile devices, so depending on the size and structure of your campaign, you could be throwing away a considerable amount of money every day on clicks that do exactly nothing for your business. One of our former clients informed us that we didn't need to worry about mobile because there was already a mobile solution in place for the site. That mobile solution was a mobile enabled site that worked decently for phones that were-compatible. However, the automatic redirect on the site that detected whether you were visiting the site from a desktop or a phone wasn't picky about how smart that phone was and just sent every visitor to the mobilesite, even if the device had a full Internet browser. If this wasn't enough, that redirect wasn't smart enough to send you to the landing page you were supposed to arrive at originally; instead, it would just send you to the home page of the "mobile version" page, where you had to start your session from the beginning, on your mobile device, while driving at full speed (you know who you are, and don't ever do this). Needless to say, this was a really bad user experience and one that was costing the company hundreds of dollars a day.

This is an extreme case, but not a rare one. Most of the time, a quick visit to one of the many tools that can be found online that will replicate the browsing experience of your site on a variety of cell phones is enough to show our clients that they are wasting their money by sending traffic from mobile devices to their sites. Sure, your site looks lovely back at the office, but it's a multicolored blur on your mobile phone.

Not Everybody Has Your Phone

Do you use any Flash-based creatives or other fancy ways to get your message across? Ever see what an iPhone does to Flash? While you're checking, here's some fun math to review: There are about 55.7 million smartphone subscribers here in the United States, give or take a few hundred thousand. At last count, the iPhone's market share of those subscribers was just shy of 25 percent. Sure, that means that there is a large percentage of folks who can render Adobe Flash on their phone, but it still means that there are almost 14 million people out there who will just see a cute little box with a question mark in the middle when they try to look at that brilliant piece of Flash that kid in the art department worked on for months.

We know it's fun to work in percentages to make yourself feel better, but 14 million people would be about the population of Beijing that just moved on to another site because you didn't bother to send them to a page that is compatible with their phone, which is something you can do.

In fact, you can target specific smartphones and tablets, and outside the United States you can even target specific carriers. Remember that when the last consultant you had told you that you needed to split out your content network campaign on AdWords from your search campaign? Well, now you need to do that with mobile devices, too, or at the very least, you should turn that part of your campaign off completely until you have your act together.

Key Elements of Mobile Search Campaigns

Another reason to target specific phones or carriers has to do with the product you're selling. For example, if you sell mobile apps, I'm sure you know that iPhone apps don't work on an Android and vice versa. But does your paid search campaign know that? You may want to consider splitting the campaign in two and targeting each device separately and with a separate landing page (or send them directly to the appropriate app store). This also applies to the different carriers in different parts of the world. Perhaps you're in the ringtone business and need to remove the carriers that don't allow for customizable ringtones.

Your AdWords campaign is a lot more complex than you probably think it is. Take the time to look over every detail, ask yourself the hard questions, and make the tough decisions about the direction of your campaign. If you don't do this, be prepared to spend a lot of money on traffic you will never be able to use or at least be prepared to explain this to your boss when asked why you're wasting his/her budget.

Paid Search Buying Strategy

Relying exclusively on the company selling you ads for advice on buying ads is a little like heading off to the used car dealer, handing him a blank check, and asking for a fair price.

It shouldn't surprise you that "recommendations" coming from a search engine almost always suggest that spending more money will solve all of your problems. It doesn't matter where you go in the world, the sales pitch is the same. At the end of the day, you don't need a sales pitch; you need an efficient marketing strategy.

Spending more money may in fact be the solution to your problem, but it's more than likely you'll be wasting the money if you don't have a well thought-out approach.

Bringing in more money may in fact be the solution to increased revenue, but it seems every directive search advertising initiative reaches a point of diminishing returns. Returns most often manifest in a diminished capacity in the form of higher costs per desired action when scaling attempts are made. For many advertisers, getting past the invisible barrier of higher returns at an acceptable cost per action is a monumental task and a topic deserving its own strategy guide.

Social Ads and Search

A good search ad can live for months at a time. Thousands of directive search queries can be performed (or content ads delivered), and the same ad can be used as long as the landing page, keyword, and message are living in harmony. Social media ads now represent the majority of the ads seen on the web, and depending on frequency with which these ads are appearing, each ad might only last hours or a day or so.

Exhausting creative at such a high frequency is not something search marketers have a great deal of experience with. Yet, because many of third-party tools built to manage search campaigns are now used to manage

Facebook and other social ad formats, search marketers are adopting creative disciplines as the need arises.

There are no doubt similarities in paid ad formats. The check box targeting formats are very similar to search. In directive search, your target identifies itself and subsequently tells you what it wants. In Facebook, as in display advertising, it's up to you to create the need. As we speak, the tools and the enabling technology provided by Facebook continue to evolve, so keep an eye out for innovations in comparative analytics and for ways to help creative keep pace with inventory at scale.

When the world fell in love with Google, a lot of brand and agency managers felt they had to have a relationship with Google. More than a few lost track of the notion that someone selling ads might have an agenda that doesn't coincide with your brand's needs. The same thing is happening with Facebook, and it's sad to watch folks fall prey to the relationship syndrome. You must understand that a one sided "relationship" with the person selling you ads whose only incentive is to sell you more ads, isn't a healthy relationship.

It has never been easier for a media seller to exploit its brand equity with advertisers than it is now for Facebook and Google.

Just because a new ad format is introduced and you feel like someone has given you a great "opportunity" to buy ads you should not necessarily buy them. It never ceases to amaze me when a brand endorses a publisher's ad unit with a case study that's broadcast to anyone who'll listen. It's just like a celebrity endorsement for a product, except in lieu of a check the endorser gets a lava lamp and a handshake. Then again, if there is a check, there might be a bigger problem. The media seller gets a big bonus, a larger house, and a shill. Some might call that being exploited.

For now, buy the ads, but remember to keep your interests at the forefront of your buying motivations. And in the name of all things broadband, consider the source's motivations. Build your social influence infrastructure and remember that just because you buy the ads the same way, ads shouldn't be treated the same way.

CHAPTER 8

UNDERSTANDING SEARCH ENGINE OPTIMIZATION

If the search engine robots can't tell from your site what you do, they can't share it with the world.

Organic search optimization (aka SEO or natural search optimization) means modifying your site and landing page content to make it more likely that those pages appear higher on the list of the search results for relevant searches. It is referred to as "organic" because you are not paying directly for the placement.

However, SEO isn't free. The cost is significant. It is an investment of time, energy, content production, software subscriptions, and other soft costs, such as engaging social strategies to reflect the content search engines see.

When marketers start down the search path, they often ask, "Why do I need to pay for search ads if I can make my website rank for free?" Or, conversely, they wonder, "Why do I have to wait for SEO to work if I can just pay to have my ad on the top of the page now?"

Have you heard the expression "Don't put all of your eggs into one basket?"

Unless you yourself are a Goliath, it would be darn near impossible to support "always on" coverage for every search relevant to your business in both paid search and organic search.

THE TOP DOWN

You can't think about editorial search without thinking about the ads, so if you skipped over the chapter on paid ads hoping to just jump into the organic part, you should go back and read that chapter first. We'll wait.

Search engine optimization is undoubtedly the most misunderstood aspect of digital marketing. It breeds the most confusion, mythology, and dogmatic discipline seeking. It offers the least amount of control and the most speculative return measurement. It is the easiest digital marketing discipline for getting lost in the forest while looking for the trees.

If you take a step back from the day-to-day pursuit of sophisticated algorithmic shifts (known as "dances" to the insiders) and take a broader look at natural search, you find the basic dynamics of earning your place in search results have not changed much in the last decade.

The need to be "seen" by search engines hasn't changed.

The need to be relevant to the searchers expressed intent hasn't changed.

The need for human searchers to validate the first two dynamics hasn't changed.

So let's take a look at search engine optimization from a very basic perspective to help you build a solid marketing strategy.

THE BASIC MECHANICS

Search engines use robots to "view" information in the form of text, images, video, audio, and any other content format that will be conjured in the foreseeable future. This content is then categorized or filed, so that it can be connected to defined interest categories or keywords. The content also undergoes a reference or background check to see if other people like the content. This is commonly referred to as "link equity." You can think of these links or references the same way you think of interviewing for a job. The more powerful the reference, the greater the weight assigned to the candidate. Essentially, search rankings aren't any more complicated than that.

There is a mountain of information on the importance of and the association with art and science as it relates to a successful SEO strategy.

However, the cold harsh reality of most failed or flawed SEO strategies has nothing to do with a lack of knowledge. Modern failures have nothing to do with a lack of understanding of the process. Flawed strategies have nothing to do with the all too popular references to algorithmic shifts or the failure to keep up with them. It's been nearly ten years since the first enterprise SEO book was released, and we still see some very common errors occurring at a very high frequency. To say that any of these errors would be easy to avoid would be an oversimplification of the problem.

When it comes to the concepts of content and links in connection with search engine optimization, it's easy to fall into the trap of quantity over quality. Perhaps it's the fault of the optimizers who aren't specific enough when speaking of what practices can get a site moved up in the organic ranks of search engines. Maybe it's the fault of the search engines themselves for not plugging such an obvious loophole in the algorithms they use to determine which sites are the most relevant for certain terms. Or perhaps it's the site owners who are trying to find the shortcut to the front of the pack.

The truth is that no matter who is to blame, the days of intentionally or unintentionally abusing the rules of content and links are quickly coming to a close as more and more big brands are being caught in the act of trying to game the rules of search engine optimization. At the end of the day, the content of a site or page is what really matters.

CONTENT: IT'S NOT A QUANTITY GAME

Content is important. But like most other things, too much of anything can cause some real problems.

You won't be able to begin your search engine journey without coming across the term "content farm." Search engines adjust their algorithms to bury the pages of so-called content farms or block some of them outright. The issue that the search engines and many industry pundits have with content farms is that the latter have not only taken advantage of a chink in the search engine algorithm armor but are also very good at doing so.

The concept is quite simple: the content farms either manually or sys-temically analyze search data for the most popular terms and then assign writing staff to create new content to match these terms so that their site appears in the search results. This (quite often) low-quality and low-cost content is surrounded by advertising, which is sometimes even provided by the search engines themselves. The content farms make money, the search engines make money, and everybody is happy—everybody except the legitimate businesses that actually deserve to rank higher in search engine results because their content is far more relevant than what the content farms are churning out. Now, with more and more content farms figuring out automated ways to mine data for more and more content to create, the results for the most popular terms on the web are becoming more and more flooded with poor quality content with nothing but advertising at its heart.

How does this most recent witch hunt affect you and your site? Content farms have forced search engines to create more aggressive methods of dealing with the massive content flow. You will regularly hear about "updates" to the algorithmic decision-making process of evaluating what constitutes valuable content. These updates from search engines are given cute animal names (for example, Google's Panda update) and often incite panic in the hearts of site owners everywhere. The good news is that the low-quality content that was created solely for the sake of spamming the search engines is slowly disappearing from view; the bad news is that if your site was even just accidentally participating in this practice, it will suffer a ding in rankings together with the content farms.

The solution is, of course, to stay out of the low-quality content game entirely. As Internet marketing consultants, we have seen our fair share of clients who never meant to be the owners of poorly made content, but they are now owners of it just the same. Often clients are surprised to discover that less than ethical SEO firms develop content to garner positions that aren't related to their business. Sure, the pages ranked well for certain terms and created new traffic for the business' site, but the exit rate for those visitors was well over 90 percent without so much as a whiff of brand purchase intent. This translates into hours of wasted development time and money, all in the name of "more content gets you more traffic."

Site owners who are putting resources toward the generation of new site content to increase organic traffic would be wise to analyze their strategy and the resulting content to make sure that the content created lines up with the goals of the business. Furthermore, site owners should take the time to review the exit rates of existing content to determine whether that content is functioning as intended or is simply creating worthless traffic to their site.

Like anything else of value, content creation requires a process to optimize its outcome. Quality site content doesn't magically happen but is generally the result of using campaign feedback to make decisions regarding content placement and key words and to reevaluate who the site is trying to communicate with.

SEO isn't a campaign. It's more like planting a garden. While you may figure out how to drop the seeds in the ground, there's a lot more to gardening than that. Over time the seedlings need to be watered, weeds need to be pulled, and the right combination of sun and rain is crucial to the process.

However, unlike a garden, the SEO process does not depend on luck to move forward if we take key steps such as the following along the way:

- Audit your existing web pages and create a road map that can take you where you want to go. Let's agree that despite your best efforts and the absolute genius of the people who create your web page there is still room for improvement. The basic acid test is one of determining what purposes you really want your pages to accomplish. Is yours just an information site or are there points of conversion that you want to increase? How do you expect your site to evolve? What long-term sales goals are you reaching for?

- Welcome input from all stakeholders. A single perspective cannot be universal. While you may work with some of the smartest people in your industry, you still need to reach out at times to others who can offer a different perspective. It's amazing how much you can learn just by asking the right questions.

- Evaluate whether you have the internal resources to reach your goals. Look, the harsh reality of most businesses is that there is always a limited amount of time, money, or both. It's great to have goals, but if you can't actually reach them because of a lack of resources, then that can be a special kind of hell. Instead, evaluate what needs to be done and weigh it against the resources you have on hand. This may mean that instead of accomplishing everything you want to in one fell swoop, you might have to reach toward your goals in smaller steps as resources become available.

- Combine all available data from benchmarks. Have you been able to determine what's already working well? Do you have pages that are getting a lot of visits or pages that are converting well? Use that existing understanding as a line in the sand that you can use to determine whether future efforts are performing better or worse than past efforts. Again, the goal is to move forward as much as possible. By asking the right questions and being open to the answers, especially if they're not overly flattering, you can gain deep insights into what's working for you and what actions you can take to fix what is currently not working well.

- Redraw your road map and focus on the tasks that take the least amount of time and money to implement but can yield the greatest increase in results. There's nothing wrong with going after the low-hanging fruit. Sometimes simple things, such as editing web pages to include words that are more in line with those prospects are using to find your web sites and landing pages, can yield huge results. Not everything you do to increase exposure has to be resource intensive or require a PhD. Again, by identifying what's working and what isn't you're already way ahead of most of your competitors.

LINKS: NOW THAT YOU'VE SEEN WHAT DAMAGE CAN BE DONE

You can't blame the *New York Times* for a headline like this: "The Dirty Little Secrets of Search." After all, the audience for the article that exposed how JCPenney had for years been using various forms of link spam to garner higher search results for a myriad of terms was pretty broad. But the truth is that the black hat practices described in the article that appeared that quiet Sunday morning were neither "little" nor a "secret" but were, without a doubt, very "dirty."

What search sites often call "link schemes" is pretty clear. A site should never deal with links that exist for no other reason than to attempt to manipulate search results. You should also avoid the following bad habits:

1. Avoid web spammers soliciting large quantities of links
2. Similarly, avoid companies offering to exchange links in large quantities
3. Finally, you should never deal with companies that are buying or selling links that "pass PageRank."

You needn't read every SEO guide or best practices document provided by a search engine or a third party to sort out what constitutes what common sense tells you is a bad idea. Remember that SEO strategy is a long-term (Figure 8.1) game.

Yet, in a moment of desperation and heavy pressure to meet quarterly numbers, someone in upper management may ask one of the younger

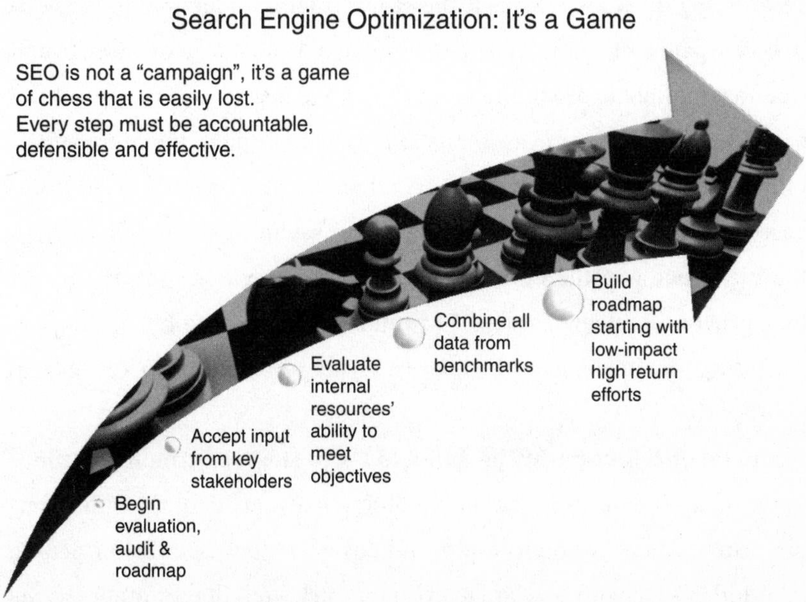

Search Engine Optimization: It's a Game

SEO is not a "campaign", it's a game of chess that is easily lost.
Every step must be accountable, defensible and effective.

Begin evaluation, audit & roadmap

Accept input from key stakeholders

Evaluate internal resources' ability to meet objectives

Combine all data from benchmarks

Build roadmap starting with low-impact high return efforts

Figure 8.1   Search charts

members of the marketing team if anyone "knows a guy" who can help the company goose its organic traffic…just for a little while until the real stuff falls into place. The real issue at this point isn't that you just broke one of search's golden rules, but that breaking that rule actually works, at least for a little while. That is, it works until you are either directly or indirectly outed, or until you do it so much that a search engine (or the *New York Times*) can't help but notice that you're abusing the system and takes you and your listings down a peg in a big and showy way. At that point, you can only hope that you don't end up the subject of an exposé article on bad SEO practices and that you may keep your job for a little while longer.

At search marketing conferences, one of the featured and favorite panels is usually one that now usually takes place during the cocktail hour or at a pub, namely, the infamous face-off of black hat versus white hat. As fun as these sessions are to watch each year, we all know they're probably not helping things. While most attendees of those sessions are taking careful notes to avoid just about every trick the representatives of the dark arts have to offer, there are always a few folks who cross over to the dark side that night. The lure of the quick and easy path to the power of the purchased link is just too tempting, the arguments just too strong.

Among those arguments is the philosophical discussion of just what makes a paid link these days. Not long ago, Overstock.com was penalized for trading big discounts for links from .edu domains for the sake of better results. However, Google itself engaged in one of the more widely known instances of a similar practice when it gave bloggers free Android-based phones for reviewing the operating system upon launch. Perhaps the difference was the domains targeted by Overstock.com or the fact that providing review copies of products isn't new at all, but still, it is confusing for site owners who are just trying to get a little link love from another site.

In the end, the best defense is not to tempt fate at all. Among the thousands of articles on white-hat link building that can be found with a simple search, you're bound to find hundreds of methods purely for getting inbound links to your site. You'll no doubt catch a few of the authors trying their best to sound like the bad boys of search by instructing you on how to steal links from your competitors or hunt for dead links on .edu domains, both of which are legitimate methods and won't get you in trouble with the search engine spam monitors.

Practical Wisdom—Before Google was a household name and the single dominant entity in the seek-and-find digital world, search engines consisted of far more than one or two websites that guided people to content. When search engines began to automate their indexing systems, they began to use software applications called "bots" (short for "robots") to gather information. These bots visit websites and gather information and report back to their search engines, millions of times faster than humans could. Indeed, search sites wouldn't exist as we know them today without these bots. Many IT departments justifiably considered these indexing bots to be invasive intruders and went to great lengths to block them. Remember, every time a human being visits a site, that human uses some of the site's bandwidth or resources. As more people go to a website, more bandwidth is needed to keep pages loading fast and traffic moving. Bots use up precious bandwidth the same way people do and that can be a problem. From the IT manager's perspective, there are hundreds or thousands of these bots constantly crawling through their websites. Many of these bots ignore commonly held standards of not accessing a site's content, and IT managers have to aggressively block them because the bots slow sites down and negatively impact the experience humans have on websites.

In the not-so-distant past, one such bot that was new to the scene was the aptly named Google Bot. Google Bot demanded a great deal of bandwidth from a major brand's website so the solution IT deployed (without consulting marketing) was to simply block Google Bot. As you might imagine, blocking Google Bot had a negative effect on site traffic. Eventually the problem was discovered, and it was explained that Google was a good bot and had to be allowed back on the site.

Since then, major advances have been made in communications between bots and site owners, but there are a couple of lessons to be learned here. First, you can't operate in isolation: communicating efforts across all departments is essential to achieving companywide goals. Second, while healthy skepticism is good, technology advances rapidly, and many people can't keep up. Rapid changes affect your efforts in ways you may not readily consider. Simply shutting something off can have dire consequences; therefore, you have to remain vigilant and stay informed.

CHAPTER 9

THE SOCIAL MEDIA UNIVERSE

Social media can easily connect brands and consumers. That doesn't always make for an easy relationship.

While the evolution of the World Wide Web dramatically changed the way we do business and gain access to information, it was the arrival of social media that really started to change how we all interconnect. In short, social media platforms were able to give us quick and immediate access to one another.

The idea of online social media isn't new. Back in the early 1990s, before the earliest web browsers arrived, millions of people found ways to connect with one another online using what they called BBSs (bulletin board systems). There early information repositories allowed users to connect to a single computer or server (generally using phone lines and a modem) that stood as an information hub. Users could upload and download files as well as post messages on the boards. In a number of ways the model served very much like a clubhouse.

These early social media hubs experienced many of the same challenges that more developed social media channels face today: trolls, flame wars, inappropriate postings, etc. But these sites also ushered in the promise of cooperative development, meaningful socialization between people divided by geography, an opportunity to ask questions and learn from other people, and at the core of it all, the ability to share anything and everything.

Here we explore the dynamics of this interconnected world and how this ability to share has changed the very fabric of human societies around the world. While we certainly acknowledge the popularity and significance of many of the social media platforms, such as Facebook, Twitter, Pinterest, Wikipedia, LinkedIn, YouTube, Instagram, eBay, and Amazon along with the continuous arrival of new and innovative ways to connect people with one another, we're purposefully taking an agnostic approach to the different technologies and methodologies and instead focus more on helping you understand and develop the different social media marketing strategies that can be used to effectively communicate the value and opportunities your business represents.

Social media is about bringing people together in a mutually beneficial way. Once again, it doesn't require deep pockets or even a marketing budget to be effective using most social media channels. In a lot of ways, the Davids embracing social media have an advantage over the Goliaths because they can move faster and more decisively. Too many Goliaths have layers of complexity built into their infrastructures, and this often means that before any missive from the company gets in front of the public it first needs to be blessed by a legal, marketing, or HR department or all of them. That message then often arrives at the party well after everybody else.

But at its core social media success is about being innovative and learning how to create or join conversations at the right time. It's about creating engaging ways to communicate value and to give people the tools and understanding they need to interact with one another. Social media also represent a way to give every person on earth the ability to share his or her opinions, thoughts, dreams, plans, insights, and pictures of their cats with other people who find this information interesting and valuable.

Social media represent a huge paradigm shift in how the masses communicate and are communicated with. Unlike their mass marketing predecessors, social media aren't based on a voice of authority paradigm. Instead, social media are driven by the collective experience. The information being presented is decentralized and largely organic. Social media are about a collective experience and only work through participation and interaction with others.

Perhaps the most significant thing is that nobody is in charge of what gets shared and what doesn't (apart from decency guidelines on several platforms). Every topic under the sun is discussed and finds its audience. Every participant has an equal voice, and others are free to listen or not. Social media is a free marketplace of global ideas, perspectives, opinions, and outlooks.

Social media is also a very noisy place.

THE RISE OF THE PROSUMER

The Internet created new opportunities for marketers by letting consumers help them tell their stories.

Previously, anybody wanting to have access to mass marketing either had to have control of an existing channel or very deep pockets. The average person, whether focused on marketing a business or not, was locked out.

The rise of social media brought a level playing field to anybody who wanted a voice to share with the world. Traditional channels covering areas of print and broadcast suddenly lost their exclusivity as millions of people around the world created their own broadcast centers through the use of blogs, podcasts, and video sharing. For the first time in history, anybody who had a story to tell or something to share had global access to the other people in the world who wanted to be part of that conversation.

As social media channels evolved, the media development tools available evolved as well. Video production platforms that only a few decades ago cost upward of half a million dollars and required highly specialized skills to use gave way to the thousand-dollar TV studio consisting of a laptop computer, an affordable video camera, and editing software. Now whatever was created could be shared with a global audience. Through channels like YouTube anybody who wanted to have a television station had the freedom to create and promote his or her unique programs.

Before long, average people were equipped with a camera and video camera through their smartphones and had ready access to the Internet at any time, anywhere. This created incredible changes and shifted news gathering and reporting, for example, from being the exclusive domain of professional journalists to something ordinary people could do too.

The rise of the new broadcaster created an explosion of new information. It allowed people to share their passions, beliefs, and interests with the world and find responsive audiences. It gave ordinary people the opportunity to become extraordinary and created a whole new level of celebrity, wealth, and sharing.

The rise of the new broadcaster was significant. Current statistics put the number of active blogs worldwide at somewhere around 200 million. It is also currently estimated that roughly 72 hours' worth of video is uploaded to YouTube every minute (it's also estimated that around 300 billion hours of YouTube videos are watched every month). There are thousands and thousands of online radio stations. Channels such as iTunes host millions of hours' worth of podcasts. In short, there is no shortage of information or access to that information.

Not surprisingly, this influx of new programming created a huge fragmentation across the information landscape. With this explosion of new content and sources of news, entertainment, and information came the new marketing challenge of trying to figure out which of these new channels represented the best way to reach the right people.

SOCIAL MEDIA MARKETING

The focus of social media, as with all other forms of marketing, is to reach the right people.

The bottom line is that your message, content, and ideas are going to appeal to a specific audience. As a result, we want to leverage the social media channels and tools to create the most relevant connection between "our" audiences and our content.

In contrast to traditional mass marketing models, these new developments mean that we're not looking merely to present information to these people but instead are looking for people who are willing to participate in the conversation we are having with the marketplace. We're looking for people who need the information and benefits we offer and who are also willing to participate in the discovery of that information and share it with others.

Not surprisingly, effective social media marketing doesn't happen in a vacuum. Effective social media marketing generally ties in with other marketing efforts taking place in a company.

Not too many years ago, a number of companies embracing social media marketing for the first time created special teams whose job it was to reach out through social media channels to promote the company's brands and services. The major disconnect for many of these early experiments was in discovering that siloing social media as just another possible marketing channel often created problems and conflicts with the insights and marketing strategies being employed by traditional marketing and sales teams.

Also problematic was that a number of organizations gave lip service to the idea of social media outreach but didn't always empower the people in the organization to effectively promote and share brand insights publicly. This periodically resulted in company bloggers being called on the carpet for sharing company insights without first getting the approval of legal and/or marketing departments.

What we've come to understand during the past decade or so is that companies that speak to consumers in a human voice generally do much better. Even those of us who spend our days thinking like marketers are also consumers. Very few of us like sales pressure. Most of us also have finely tuned BS detectors that automatically filter out any suspicious or insincere sounding marketing babble. As a result, we have the tendency to distrust marketing organizations because we fully understand that they have a vested interest in telling us what they think we most want to hear.

While we won't go into the moral implications of less savory marketing practices, the one takeaway we want to share is that in social media, as in other aspects of modern business, transparency isn't just a good idea but a moral imperative. As consumers, we do business with companies we trust. As consumers, we communicate with companies we feel respect us. As consumers, we take action when we feel safe.

One of the most interesting aspects of social media in relation to consumerism is the idea behind online product reviews. While we hear stories from time to time of people being paid to write favorable reviews for books and other products, we also believe that the crowdsourcing of reviews has a chance to find a vein of truth. This means that if a company pays somebody to write a great review for a product that is subpar, they might get an initial bump in traffic or sales, but as more and more unpaid reviewers take the pulpit, their opinions will go a long way toward neutralizing anything overly fawning or optimistic. In short, if you ask enough people their true opinions, you'll eventually arrive at a consensus.

But the significance of this model is how it affects consumers. I suspect that you, like most people, have at some point in the past decade made an online buying decision based upon the comments and reviews of a total stranger. In fact, "recommendations by other people" is the number one reason driving decisions to buy. While we do not even know the people making the recommendations, their motivations, or even if we would trust them if we knew them in real life, we still have the tendency to believe more in a product review written by other consumers than we would in similar information presented by a marketer.

As we've explored several times in this book, effective marketing isn't about getting a message out to everybody, it's about getting a message to the right people. The same thing holds true for social media channels. While most social media offers users a broadcast model of sorts, it also offers a more refined way to reach people who share common interests and desires with the brand.

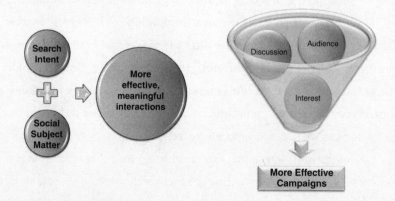

Figure 9.1   Social media examples

We look at a typical sales or marketing funnel, and we see that there is an evolution of thinking that takes place between hearing about a brand or service for the first time and becoming a customer of that brand or service. We may chalk up a lot of this evolution to marketing campaigns and sales efforts, but we also have to acknowledge that the conversations that we have with other people may have the greatest impact on what we end up buying or not buying in the future.

For example, let's say that you're in the market for a new car. Chances are that commercials and advertisements for new cars are suddenly going to appear on your personal radar. But it's also highly likely that you're going to discuss your need with friends and colleagues and solicit their advice on the types of features and performance you might want in a new car. In this context, you are actively looking for information that can help you make your decision.

There are several different types of influencers consumers come into contact with:

1. Positional influencers: these are family members or close friends who can offer trusted opinions and insights to other people trying to make a brand decision.
2. Expert influencers: these include blog owners, industry experts, professionals, brand managers, and product reviewers. These people can be found through social media channels and have often built up a meaningful level of trust among consumers.
3. Referrers: these are people who actively support a brand or product by voluntarily sharing their experiences and insights with others. This includes product reviewers and creators of social media fan sites.

For many consumers, there's not a lot of difference between influencers. They are looking for a solution to a problem and are often receptive to insights and understanding from many other people, including the brand marketers themselves. They want to feel that they made the right purchasing decision that will give them what they want or need and help them avoid buyer's remorse.

This means that savvy marketers need to be able to share their brand insights and knowledge with consumers looking for this information as much as they can. As we mentioned before, this can often be difficult because consumers don't generally trust the opinions of the advertising company because they obviously have skin in the game. But for companies willing to be honest and transparent there are some great social media opportunities available.

It's important to be aware that there is spectrum of influencers for every existing brand ranging from fans to active marketing partners. These may include existing customers, industry experts, personal friends of company employees, and even total strangers willing to share positive opinions about a brand or service.

Savvy marketers need to spend time identifying and rewarding individuals who are actively influencing others regarding their brands. This includes doing keyword searches for brand or company names so that when a company is addressed through social media channels such as blogs, twitter streams, and Facebook posts those moments of influence are being noted.

It also gives brand marketers an opportunity to reward those individuals who are active influencers. This could include acknowledging a blogger who posted positive insights about a brand or service by simply leaving a note on the blog in question to say thank you. It might also include donating promotional items such as T-shirts to a blogger with an offer to give them away as gifts and prizes to his or her readers. This simple act can grow over time to create cobranding opportunities in which a brand can reach more influencers and the target audience members through the blog. Not only do these actions validate the blogger, but they can help turn that individual channel into a strong media ally.

In other cases, brand marketers can offer special benefits to the people who are talking up the brand through social media channels. Again, full transparency is the best course of action here. This means that a blogger, a Twitterer, and a Facebook fan, and the brand marketers should all feel comfortable acknowledging any promotional consideration. It should look like friends sharing information with other friends.

Practical Wisdom—It's also important to point out that not all information shared about a brand is positive. That makes the monitoring and understanding of social media brand management even more important. If it turns out that an individual is making disparaging remarks about your brand, you need to know this is happening and be able to do whatever you can to minimize the effects of any negative branding as quickly as possible. In most cases, being able to directly approach the commenter and determine a way to help settle that person's grievances is a perfect first step.

Without going deeper into customer care philosophies, let's just agree that customers expect to be treated with respect by the companies they do business with. From time to time, there are customer care disconnects, and a consumer may walk away from the situation feeling bitter and vindictive. These same customers generally have a wide range of access to social media channels through which they can air their complaints.

Historically, consumers who felt disrespected by a company had plenty of opportunity to share their grievances with their friends and family, and the company would be none the wiser. Today, because these conversations can be located through keyword searches, companies can immediately get involved in conversations with disgruntled consumers and quickly resolve those issues.

Almost paradoxically, many companies that have successfully reached out to disgruntled former clients ended up turning negative advocates into some of their biggest brand promoters! Never underestimate the power of showing other people respect while listening to what's on their minds.

HOW TO MARKET WITHOUT MARKETING

Marketers have a huge challenge: they're generally not trusted by the very people they're trying to start conversations with.

The main challenge is that most consumers don't trust the motives of marketers because the latter obviously have a vested interest in the process and can't be objective. The bottom line is that many consumers believe that a marketer will tell them anything, even if it's not true, in order to make a sale.

The solution to this problem is often to step away from sounding like a marketer by writing from a human perspective. This may sound odd, but in many cases "marketing speak" tries to rise above its humanity by creating an overly enthusiastic and not very realistic picture of what a product or service can mean to consumers. Consider television commercials that use the "but wait, there's more!" format of marketing. While it may be a useful approach for grabbing people's attention and inspiring them to take action, this promotional approach can also take a nosedive if the hype doesn't live up to the reality. More often than not, consumers seeing an ad for a miracle product on television are going to do a quick search online to get a better sense of whether an offer is snake oil or whether previous buyers of the product have nice things to say about their purchases.

For savvy marketers this means learning to speak in a human voice again. It means that as marketer you have to express a willingness to be transparent and genuine. You don't always want to represent the voice of authority. In some cases you just want to be a friend sharing an incredible opportunity with them.

Also, being human means that you don't need to hide your flaws from others. Human beings make mistakes and companies that are willing to admit that they had a misjudgment or did something wrong often garner the trust of consumers more quickly.

A great example of this is the Domino's Pizza "Turnaround" TV commercial that first aired in 2009. Company president Patrick Doyle appeared in these commercials and shared with the public feedback he had gotten from focus groups about the company's product. Phrases such as "the crust tastes like cardboard," "the sauce tastes like ketchup," and "the pizza is devoid of all flavor" flashed up on the screen. At first glance, it looked like marketing suicide. After all, what brand spends lots of money on TV commercials to tell customers that their product sucks? But that's exactly what they did. And in the process of opening up and sharing their flaws with the marketplace, Domino's marketers also made a promise to viewers: that they were going to start all over and create the most perfect pizza they could by introducing new ingredients and new approaches.

Did the campaign have a positive impact? The first quarter of 2010 was one of the company's best earnings quarters ever; Domino's experienced a 14.3 percent increase over the fourth quarter of 2009. In addition, the company's stock rose by 130 percent, which was one of the highest ever revenue jumps for a fast food chain. Today Dominos is the second largest pizza chain in the world and the fourth largest e-tailer in the United States (sharing the dais with Amazon, Staples, and Office Depot). Yes, it worked.

While plenty of credit can be given to the business planning behind the campaign, the main impact of the campaign was based on the refreshing honesty of a company sharing what plenty of their consumers already knew and making a promise to make things better. They did and consumers responded favorably. It was a very human (and smart!) thing to do.

There is probably already a conversation about your brand and services taking place. If you're not actively trying to become part of that conversation, you're missing a huge opportunity. Here are a few ways you can track and approach mentions of your brand:

- Set up Google alerts for your company name, brand names, service marks, executives, and any other keywords that might be used with regard to your company or business (learn more at http://www .google.com/alerts). This free service allows you to scan the Internet for your chosen keyword(s) and a report will sent to your e-mail address daily or weekly. Google monitors new web content coming from news sources, blogs, web pages, videos, discussions, and books.
- Monitor the blogosphere. Sites like Technorati.com, Twingly. com, and addictomatic.com all have great features that can allow marketers to search for brand and company keywords and allow for new conversations to be found and addressed quickly.

- Make an effort to contact bloggers or journalists who mention your brands either positively or negatively. Be respectful and thank them for positive mentions. Ask respectfully if you can refute or clarify negative comments. If there's a way to share a lapse in customer care or shortsightedness on the part of the company, then do so. Just remember that this isn't your bully pulpit. This channel belongs to somebody else, and you are a guest. Act accordingly.

- Use a dashboard product such as Tweetdeck (tweekdeck.twitter. com) to monitor Twitter feeds using your brand and service keywords.

- Contact brand advocates directly through their social media channels. Thank them for the mention and acknowledge their patronage and help. You may be surprised how far a little kindness and recognition can go.

- Do the same for negative mentions. *Do not* attack or strive for vindication. You need to take the high road, and you need to genuinely ask how you can fix what might be broken. In most cases the disgruntled have something on their minds that wasn't resolved. If you can address the problem directly, you just might change a possible troll into a strong brand advocate.

Ultimately, our job as marketers is to create a positive relationship between our brands and our customers. If you approach your role in social media as one of making friends and managing conflicts, then you will be heading down the right path.

USING SOCIAL MEDIA FOR COMPETITIVE ANALYSIS

You should always know what your competitors are up to.

We live in a competitive world. In a lot of ways, competition between businesses has increased during the past few decades due to increased global connectivity. In short, your competitors are no longer restricted to local markets but can be any other company worldwide that provides the same products and services you do.

In the wired world, a competitor is any other company, site, or resource that prospects or customers can turn to for advice, training, education, benefits, entertainment, and anything else they want. Today's consumers use price, ease of use, keyword searches, shipping convenience, engaging websites, and all sorts of other criteria to determine which online businesses they want to do business with.

This means that in order to stay competitive businesses not only need to be able to provide their target audience with what they want across all aspects of their online marketing, sales, and general business practices, but they also need to be fully aware of what their competitors are bringing to the marketplace and whether they represent a threat or an opportunity.

Like other aspects of social media, competitive analysis is really just keeping your eyes on what other businesses are doing by monitoring their online actions. As we discussed earlier in this chapter, using tools like Google alerts, Twitter alerts, and monitoring the blogosphere for brand names and business keywords as well as monitoring different social networks can allow any business to keep tabs on what competitors are doing. It allows marketers to remain aware of potential challenges in the marketplace and to use that understanding to help their own businesses identify their unique selling propositions (USPs) to help them stand out from the crowd.

The bottom line is that businesses need to do their due diligence in order to be aware of areas where their competitors might eat their lunch.

MAKE YOUR OWN PATH

Your brand is unique, and as such it needs to be approached and managed in a unique way.

Here's how:

One of the challenges of working in social media channels is that a lot of people are looking for recipes that will help them achieve marketing success. The problem with this thinking is that it presumes that a brand is interchangeable with any other brand.

Social media marketing gives marketers an opportunity to create a targeted and meaningful conversation with the right people. These are prospects, existing customers, and influencers. Part of what makes social media work is standing out from the crowd. If you do exactly what every other brand marketer is doing in order to stand out, then the conclusion is obvious: you end up hiding in plain sight.

Instead, you want to make some meaningful noise on social media channels. Again, we're not talking about being loud and obnoxious. We're talking about being interesting and engaging and standing out from the crowd because you are offering something unique and intriguing. Sometimes that message comes through in the content you post on your site and social media channels and those of other people. At other times, your message is based on innovatively grabbing consumers' attention by doing things in a slightly different way.

Part of what makes this work is identifying what your brand's or company's social media voice sounds like. After all, the platforms and channels that you use should be those that allow you to reach the people you most want to talk with. As we discussed in chapter 3, by identifying who we most need to reach we can start to generate meaningful conversations that address the needs and expectations of those people. Depending on the communication goals of the company this may include prospects and existing customers, companies, and buyers involved in a specific industry or even campaigns that address the needs of in-house staff or employees.

You also want to add value to the conversations that are taking place online. This includes creating interesting and meaningful conversations through your own social media channels, such as Facebook and Twitter. But it also means finding conversations that are taking place about your brands and services and joining them in a polite and respectful way. This includes thanking people who have posted comments that are favorable to your brands on blogs and other social network channels and also taking a professional approach to people who may have a less than favorable view of your brands and services. In those cases it is important to get involved in the conversation quickly before something just smoldering turns into a raging fire. By asking people who have written about any aspect of your brand to tell you what you can do to help them, you cannot only make a difference in the eyes of that person but also in the eyes of anybody else who ends up reading the comments. Remember, you're in the business of solving problems.

It's also worth pointing out that in many cases you may run into somebody who has an ax to grind but who really is looking for resolution. Our advice is to always take the high road here. Even if you reached out to help somebody several times and they keep slapping your hand away, stay cool and professional. You don't want to feed the trolls. However, you may find that as you approach people and try to turn negative events positive, other members of the social media community may come to your aid. There are many cases in which the disgruntled have eventually been called out by other members of the community for their negative behaviors.

After defining your target audience, you can then figure out where these people are hanging out. By thinking like your customers, you can start to approach the web by using keywords that would be consistent with the people you most want to talk to. This way you can discover and explore blogs that address the needs and interests of this audience and find individuals who are active and regular users of blogs, news feeds, and industry information sites. Then you can find which of these people are researchers and which are shoppers.

Again, sources like technorati.com can provide a lot of insight into the different blogs that cover different topics of interest to your industry and consumers.

Sometimes developing a social media voice means turning inward to do a self-assessment; for example, when people find your brand online, either through your website or through your social media channels, what perceptions about your company and its ability to solve their problems do they take away? In short, are you as cool as you hope you are?

There are a number of great online tools that will allow marketers to do a social media marketing voice self-assessment. Searching for "social media monitor" tools will give you access to a wide range of paid and free services that can monitor your social media presence across different tools and channels. Here's a short list of some of our favorites:

- Klout: Klout is a website and mobile app that uses social media analytics to rank its users according to online social influence via the "Klout Score," which is a numerical value between 1 and 100.
- Marketing Grader: Owned by Hubspot, Marketing Grader is a unique website analysis tool that takes a holistic look at a company's web presence by analyzing its web site's SEO values, social media links, mobile capabilities, and overall site structure and gives it a score and a full list of feedback on areas that can be improved.
- Hootsuite: Hootsuite is a dashboard-based monitoring service that allows marketers to integrate all of their social media channels into one feed to make monitoring easier. There is a low-end free version of the service and a more robust paid service available.
- Addictomatic: Despite its odd name, this is one of the most robust social media keyword search engines out there. Its dashboard allows users to scan blogs, social media channels, news channels, and more for specific keywords.

CHAPTER 10

THE MOBILE MARKETING CONUNDRUM

Mobile channels are exploding and creating huge opportunities for marketers. Unfortunately, many of those opportunities are hiding.

The simple reality is that the rapid development of mobile devices is changing the entire playing field of human communication. From the freedom of being untethered from largely stationary computers to the ability to have easy access to information virtually anywhere and near instantaneous communication with nearly anybody—all this is not a minor shift. Unlike traditional media and even the early Internet, mobile isn't about how people consume media but about how they interact with one another and with marketers.

Despite all this amazing growth and incredible promise, there are no clear paths for marketers to effectively communicate with consumers using mobile channels. This isn't to say that there haven't been many attempts to create advertising and marketing channels that utilize cell and smartphones, tablets and e-readers, but the challenge has been the creation of effective ways to create a meaningful conversations that resonate with mobile consumers.

We don't intend to throw the cheerleading pom-poms down on the ground completely, but we think it's only realistic to point out that mobile advertising is still a hard nut to crack. In a lot of ways the channel is so new that it is hard for us to point out definite strategies you need to consider when reaching these audiences.

Let's back up for a moment: one of the big challenges that we all face in this industry is that mobile is neither a methodology nor a channel. Instead, it's a platform that allows users access to information. For all intents and purposes, the smartphone has replaced the desktop computer as the primary way many people access the web. Obviously, this change gives users a lot more flexibility in when and how they use the web to get information they want and need. This development also changes ease-of-use parameters because a computer screen just has a lot more space to present information compared to the smartphone. That is, in exchange for flexibility and convenience, mobile users have had to give up on faster web access and larger screens. For now.

Perhaps the biggest obstacle for marketers is how mobile users perceive their devices. In short, very few people who own a smartphone think of it as a little computer they carry around. Instead, most consumers ascribe a much more personal meaning to these devices, a meaning that can almost universally be defined as "my life." Think about it. Most people who own a smartphone are within arm's length of their device during nearly every waking moment of their lives. This may look like obsessive behavior, but most of us who use a smartphone understand that this little device has become our lifeline to everybody we know and everything we want and need most days.

At the core of this paradigm shift is how we define mobile. Once upon a time, we were really excited about the prospect of being able to make a phone call without having to be at home or in an office. Early 'portable' phones were roughly the size of a large brick and generally needed a power supply robust enough to keep them going; this was usually an equally large battery pack. As a result, most early cell phones found their home in people's cars. And as cool as it might have been (and it certainly was a status symbol for some) to have a phone in your car, you were still limited to making calls only at home, in your car, or in your office.

Then the portability of cell phones changed the world. The ability to walk down the street or through a mall while talking to a friend or colleague on the phone was revolutionary at the time. It was also pretty expensive. But this process started the evolution of mobility. The idea that we could have connectivity with other people whenever it was most convenient to us changed the very fabric of society. Suddenly, we had the ability to stand in a supermarket and phone home to check on what ingredients we needed to pick up for dinner. And we could have the security of knowing that we had access to medical and emergency personnel 24/7. And we could chat with friends, family, and colleagues from really unusual places.

Today we still use the term "phone" to identify these devices, but in reality they've evolved far past the idea of being just a device that we use to call other people. In truth, depending on your age, the phone part of the device might be the least useful feature to you. Communications through texting, picture sending, social media channels, and even e-mail have given all of us near instant access to everybody else around the clock. Voice chat is optional.

These devices have also become our cameras and our video cameras. They've become our music players, our personal organizers, our dictaphones, our GPS, and our entertainment and video watching stations. In just a few years they have become "our lives" wrapped up in one tiny package. They empower us to share our thoughts and ideas with anybody who wants them. They even allow all of us to act as citizen broadcasters and to cover news events worldwide almost as soon as they happen.

Today the plethora of applications that allow us to do just about everything we want is amazing, and because these devices and applications have become such a big part of our lives, they've also become very personal.

And that's part of the problem.

Let's say that a total stranger walked up to you on the street and asked to borrow your telephone for a moment to make a call because his phone battery had died. What would your initial reaction be? Chances are if it was just a phone you were lending, you wouldn't have an issue with helping somebody out. But our phones are so much more than that now. They are the repositories of our lives. In many ways, they are the most private things we own, and we have the tendency to guard that privacy. In a lot of ways letting a stranger borrow our phones seems on a par with a stranger asking to borrow our bed to take a nap!

Because we think of our mobile devices as being so very personal we also feel reluctant to have total strangers in the form of advertisers use these devices to try to sell us things. That just feels invasive.

As a result, the early days of mobile advertising were fraught with a lot of pushback from consumers. As we will explore in this chapter, there is more than one reason why mobile advertising has failed to find a strong foothold in the mobile realm. The personalization of these devices is only one challenge. The other reason may have a lot more to do with the overall efficacy of digital display advertising and a deeper understanding of the psychology behind consumerism.

THE UNDENIABLE GROWTH OF MOBILE

Mobile growth in the form of new devices and software is ginormous. But that's not helping marketers to reach mobile audiences.

Mobile is growing rapidly. While we could shower you with lots of statistics and projections surrounding that growth, let's just agree that more and more people are finding the freedom of mobile devices to be a must-have. We know from our own habits that apart from almost instantaneous communication with others, we are also finding that devices like tablets are becoming synonymous with entertainment centers. Spider, who doesn't even own a television set at the time of this writing, watches more video programming on his iPad than he probably ever did on a television when he had one. Obviously, this blend of old media and new media still has a way to go, but it's pretty obvious that this convergence is happening and before too long it will be hard to find the dividing line between a personal computer, mobile device, and television.

Today, over 80 percent of Americans have a mobile phone with nearly 60 percent of those users using smartphones. Phones and tablets aren't the only devices out there either. Wireless-enabled devices, such as the Apple iTouch and e-readers, have flooded the market as well. There are even plenty of smart appliances that now connect directly to the web in order to communicate with and be controlled by their owners. Before long, "smart" will be everywhere.

For marketers this growth also represents incredible opportunities. But as we've already pointed out, in this new world advertising and marketing approaches are often limited, and some are fairly weak. On the other hand, mobile devices have created new channels for marketing and communication including social media channels and opt-in text messaging. These channels also allow marketers to ask for and receive almost instantaneous feedback on campaigns. Because of the dynamic nature of the mobile web, information can also be shared quickly by consumers and marketers to allow people to react immediately to need-driven campaigns.

Perhaps at the core of the mobile marketing growth are branded applications. While these applications represent utility (or entertainment in many cases), they can also become effective ways of sharing brand value with consumers. They can also serve as a direct communications link between an advertiser and consumers. This is no small thing. As recently as ten years ago, the idea of companies creating a direct access channel between themselves and their customers was virtually unheard of. Obviously, there were toll-free telephone numbers and even mailing addresses that consumers with concerns or complaints could access, but the idea of companies hanging out with their customers at their level and asking them for feedback is fairly new.

But this is not where the development started. Not surprisingly, early mobile marketers looked at the growing adoption of cell phones as a way to reach a new type of audience. While the number of consumers using cell phones was growing rapidly, most marketers couldn't easily get past the early gatekeepers, such as the technology companies Verizon, Sprint,

T-Mobile, and AT&T. In short, if marketers wanted to play, then they had to pay for access to what were essentially private networks. Add to that a multitude of different types of phones and devices, and you ended up with a jumble of options that made it nearly impossible for marketers to reach consumers.

Then a few years ago Apple, Inc., changed the playing field by doing an end-run around the telephony companies. They created a device that didn't require a gated community to be effective but instead tapped into the regular web for access to everything people could get from their desktop and laptop computers. But now this content was portable. In short, Apple built a very small and very powerful portable computer that used different types of software programs to do some very powerful and desired things for consumers.

Not only did this breakthrough allow consumers access to a greater mobile experience but it started creating a new platform for advertisers to explore, a platform that offered access nearly anywhere. Once the Google Android platform became established, that access became pretty much unlimited.

Today there are fundamentally two mobile platforms that dominate the marketplace (and their positions look very similar to those of Apple and Microsoft Windows OS of yesteryear). This has made it much easier for mobile ad networks to be created, apps to be designed and built, and devices to become more standardized. Still, the problems marketers face often have little to do with the technology driving the devices.

FINDING OPPORTUNITIES IN THE MIDST OF PROBLEMS

Consumers control their mobile reality from the apps they install to the web sites they visit. This will never change back.

In truth, things have never been better for consumers. Unlike buyers in the era of mass media when marketing messages were designed to be delivered to anybody who had access to that media channel, today's consumers can be more selective and interact directly with brands through online web sites, ads, videos, and other media resources. This level of control means that consumers have more opportunities to choose the brands they want to engage with, and they are generally more responsive to the marketing messages they are offered.

This new paradigm has made it very difficult for marketers still accustomed to one-size-fits- all marketing approaches to get much traction. The Goliath marketing mentality often does poorly in channels where marketing is limited to reaching only those people who want to be reached. Again, almost all marketing campaigns today can be designed around the idea of reaching the right people rather than as many people as possible. The reality is that in a world of options, choice, and opportunities anything that doesn't resonate as being relevant just doesn't get processed by the human brain. In short, if the message doesn't have any personal meaning for the recipient, it's processed as noise or, perhaps worse, never even seen.

This brings us to one of the critical paths that today's digital advertisers have to face: what is the best way to engage consumers on their own terms so that they will find marketing messages relevant? The answer is simple to understand and incredibly difficult to implement: attach that message to something that already provides value.

While we hope this doesn't generate a letter writing campaign looking for our heads on a platter, we are about to slaughter another sacred cow: Display ads in mobile channels don't work. People don't click on them. The engagement rates are low, and the click-through rate is lower. There are plenty of large companies rolling out mobile ad networks as we write this. They're projecting huge revenues, and they will get them. Initially. From advertisers like you. But your results are still going to be disappointing because of one simple reality: consumers don't want your message interrupting them, and they certainly don't want to leave what they're already doing to go do what you want them to do. Furthermore, so many advertisers do such a bad job of focusing on and managing conversion that most click-throughs are meaningless anyway.

Sorry. We really want to tell you that the money being spent to run mobile ads is a good bet and that you should do it. Instead, we're going to caution you against buying space ads to try to reach mobile consumers because you'd have a better shot at getting ROI for your marketing dollars if you stopped by your local casino's roulette wheel and let all your money ride on red.

Most of the stats coming out for responsiveness of mobile display ads show that a high percentage of click-throughs comes about as the result of fat-fingered consumers trying to close ad windows or accidentally touching the part of the screen where the ads reside. This isn't a strategy, and any click-throughs that occur by accident don't count. Period.

Now here's the good news: you don't need to run clickable display ads on people's phones to be successful in mobile marketing. There are lots of other and better ways to gain consumers' attention that don't require trying to interrupt them in their other tasks.

Here are a few strategies marketers wanting to make an impact in the mobile environment should consider:

Define and Deliver what YOUR Mobile Audience Most Wants and Needs

Yes, we do sound like a broken record. As much as we all might like to believe that what we sell is something that everybody would want to buy, it isn't. The people you are trying to reach with your messages are unique and have a unique problem that they want solved. You're not going to reach everybody. Ever.

Your audience is going to be largely self-selected based on those needs and based on how consumers use their mobile devices. For example, a younger demographic may be more receptive to messaging coming through text and image-sharing applications while an older group may be more responsive to an article or video exploring ways you can help them. Either way, the path you choose is very largely dependent on meeting the needs of the people you most need to get to see your message.

The bottom line is that before jumping on the latest, greatest trend in mobile marketing you still need to do your due diligence to determine just who you're trying to have a conversation with in the first place.

Mobile Offers Audience Targeting Tools Unavailable on Most Other Platforms

Because most carriers know specific information about their subscribers that information can be used to help better determine consumers' needs. In a lot of cases the information is still based on demographics and may be useful in helping better target consumers based on gender, age, and geographic markers.

However, today's smartphone technology also relies heavily on GPS as a way of determining the current location of mobile users and then leveraging that understanding to help provide a more relevant and meaningful information exchange. For example, a mobile user who lives in the Boston area doesn't want or need a list of Boston's best restaurants if he or she is in Cleveland at the time of using a search engine. In a lot of ways, with mobile users every search is a local search.

Done Right, Text Messaging Can Still Deliver Big Impact

Text messaging is no longer the domain of teenagers who seem to have a fear of talking to one another on the phone. Today text messaging is still a powerful way to allow consumers quick and easy access to information they want. For example, savvy real estate agents have learned how to place signs in front of properties they are selling and encourage home buyers driving past to text keywords to numbers in exchange for immediate access to data about the house for sale. Not only does this provide consumers with the information they want when they want it but it also allows the real estate agents access to collected phone numbers so that they can take advantage of follow-up sales opportunities.

Texting models have also been used effectively to allow consumers easy and quick access to sharing their information. The Fox television show *American Idol* has been a great case study in how to use this technology to allow viewers to vote for their favorite singers during a season. Again, this participation leaves behind a database that marketers may take advantage of.

All that said, we're not huge fans of marketers sending texts directly to consumers. We don't believe it's effective and generally garners poor results because it's disruptive, annoying, and creates a negative response of consumers to brands. These are all things that your brand probably wants to stay away from.

Branded Apps and Marketing through Apps Offers Great Opportunities

Apps offer marketers great ways to make direct connections with consumers. At the most basic level, the theme of the app can be a strong indicator of the needs of a consumer. In a lot of ways, apps represent unique channels through which consumers with unique needs and interests can be reached. For example, an app such as an investment tool or a physical fitness tool says an awful lot about the needs and interests of the person who downloaded and installed that app. In a lot of ways this presents a perfect opportunity for advertisers whose products and services address those areas of the market to get their messages directly in front of the people who are going to be most responsive.

Of course, the apps themselves can be marketing tools that create a meaningful and ongoing relationship with the consumer who installs them. In this way, by playing games, accessing information, or being productive, the consumer perpetually reinforces a brand.

DON'T CREATE AN APP JUST BECAUSE EVERYBODY ELSE IS DOING IT

One of the advantages of working in any industry for long time is that you start to see the same things cycling through again and again. In the mid-1990s CD-ROMs were the craze. Everybody had an application or product that they were putting on CD-ROM so they could get it on a store shelf where it would make millions of dollars. Let's just say that there is often a pretty harsh dividing line between what we want and what we get.

We're seeing the same kind of land grab with apps. Everybody wants to create an app that will make him or her a rich mobile superstar. And while we're not here to crush anybody's dreams, we're also aware of the odds of becoming the next mobile marketing star and feel that slow and steady is the best approach in this area.

There have been too many companies that have created mobile apps as either a way of keeping up with their competitors or in hopes of making a market impact, but their apps have fallen seriously short of the mark. Ultimately, having an app with your brand on it isn't the goal. Instead, your goal is to create value for your consumers. What matters is to create tools and pathways to understanding and things that are really interesting and engaging. What matters is to create value and experiences that people will want to have over and over again.

We're not saying don't create an app. We're saying create an app for the right reasons. And the best reasons are the people you most want to reach with those apps.

REMEMBER THAT MOBILE IS NOT A CHANNEL; IT'S A PLATFORM

As a platform, mobile is a really good job of bringing people and content together. Once again, these people are not all alike and are going to be receptive to different tools, approaches, content streams, and messaging. Part of your job is to identify which of these tools will do the best job of engaging and informing the people you most want to talk with. Is the best tool some sort of social media channel? Is your best choice to do something based on an app? Do your prospects thirst for some sort of knowledge or engagement?

Step away from thinking about mobile as being a strategy in itself and instead think about how the different ways that people use mobile devices can be leveraged to help you do a better job of communicating your company's unique selling proposition and value-added.

Brand Awareness Can Be a Powerful Tool through Mobile

While we may be a bit down on mobile display advertising as a direct response approach, there's still plenty of evidence that brand awareness can be significantly increased by ads that get in front of consumers and offer relevant and meaningful solutions to their problems. Obviously, the biggest challenge with any type of branding campaign is how do you measure its effectiveness? While we can certainly point at brand lift studies and view-through strategies, the bottom line is that branding is and always has been incredibly difficult to measure directly.

Still, a branding ad seen on a mobile device that doesn't get interacted with is no different from a television commercial that doesn't get interacted with or a newspaper ad or a radio spot that is perceived but not responded to. The reality is that branding ads are designed to inform over time. There's rarely an immediate and direct correlation between brand exposure and meeting an advertiser's conversion goals. To make matters even more difficult, it's nearly impossible to determine attribution (trying to determine at what point a consumer's decision to buy was directly related to advertising that person saw) in branding campaigns.

However, there is a correlation between brand advertising and consumer response even if we can't always put our finger on it. For advertisers who put their brand out there the biggest consideration is not trying to reach everybody but trying to reach the right people with the right message. It's not by accident that almost every form of advertising goes back to the idea of targeting the right audience first.

Search Is Huge in Mobile Environments

While we may not be very bullish on direct response banner ad campaigns in mobile environments, search is a very different story. In fact, there is some anecdotal evidence that because mobile users are not relegated to just sitting in front of a computer, they are much more active in using search tools to gather information as they move through the day.

Having search marketing strategies in place is paramount. In our opinion the money spent on search campaigns (accompanied with vigilant SEO practices for the site and landing page) is one of the best investments any marketer will ever make. These areas should be addressed before jumping to any display advertising or social media mobile strategies.

Your Websites Need to be Mobile Responsive

We'll be blunt—if mobile users visiting your website see the same things they would see if they were visiting your site through a browser on their laptop computers, then you're definitely not ready for prime time. The mobile surfing experience is different. The screens are generally much smaller, and despite what technology companies would like you to think, they are also slower.

The mobile surfing process should be streamlined to make it easy for your mobile site visitors to access, navigate, and understand the experience. This means that site designs should be flexible and dynamic and change to meet the specific needs of visitors whether they are arriving via smartphone, tablet, or computer.

IDENTIFY WAYS YOUR MOBILE PLATFORM CAN ENGAGE CONSUMERS

Yes, good marketing is often about a finding unique selling proposition (USP), but at other times it's about finding the gaps that exist in the current marketing process. What unique attributes can marketing through a mobile environment extend to your target audience?

We're not just talking about adding a QR code to your next print ad or sending a barrage of text messages to anybody willing to pay attention. Instead, you will want to focus on how consumers use their mobile devices and how you can use that understanding as part of your marketing strategy.

For example, you might offer point-of-purchase opportunities for mobile users to access exclusive coupons, additional information, or digital downloads and add-ons that offer a value extension. Or you could create an in-store or website scavenger hunt in which consumers snap pictures of the found objects and send them to a web address or social media channel. You could also create engaging and informational videos that allow consumers to quickly understand why they should buy product X from you and not your competitors.

Standing apart from the crowd is a good thing. Chances are that you're not just a marketer, but you're also a mobile user. This gives you a perspective and insight into the process that you personally would most like to see. What can you do to be innovative and to think about ways to make a direct connection with consumers using their mobile devices to help your brands and services to stand out from the crowd?

Mobile: A Great Platform for Measuring and Tracking Consumer Activity

Like other aspects of the Internet, the mobile platform is based on consumer interactions and not on some sort of passive advertising mechanism. In short, everything that consumers do on their mobile phones is purposeful and leaves behind a trace of that action. This means that campaigns can be more readily measured and that data can be analyzed to determine the overall efficacy and success of a campaign.

Once again, in order for any campaign to work it has to have a set and achievable goal. Once the goal is set, you need to determine how to measure whether that goal is being met. Because every campaign is different and every goal is different, there is no one way to measure the success or effectiveness of a campaign.

It's important to point out that setting campaign goals and measuring them are not separate. No goal should be set without having a reasonable way of measuring whether the goal is being met. This means that if the campaign goal is to distribute electronic coupons through text messaging, then there has to be something in place to measure what coupon redemption looks like and how many coupons need to be redeemed in order for the campaign to be considered successful.

Today, mobile marketing is largely about helping brands to stay relevant in the eyes of their prospects and consumers. It's about offering meaningful utility to people in exchange for their attention. The overriding goal is to take that attention and convert it to brand awareness and to then take brand awareness and help guide consumers toward reaching conversion goals. In the end, it's about having a good conversation that people want to listen to and participate in.

CHAPTER 11

THE LEVEL PLAYING FIELD

We hope this book ends up on your desk, coffee stained with some combination of pizza and/or salad dressing on its pages. In fact, if your copy becomes unusable due to a high mileage scenario not unlike the one with food stains described above, the publisher would be happy to replace this book at no cost to you. Just send your grape-juice-stained, gravy-soaked book back to Palgrave Macmillan, and the company will send you another one on the house. OK, well maybe that last comment was a little exaggerated, but we're sure if you send the authors a copy of your overused book along with a request for a new one, we will find it hard to say no. We'll reserve the right to exploit your extensive hard use of the book in social media with self-congratulatory posts about our super useful book.

You should be excited about the Goliath standing before you. He's clumsy, and today you have all the same weapons he has in his arsenal. Of course, one man's arsenal is another man's toolbox. You should know by now we aren't selling you "untold secrets" and *Taking Down Goliath* is not a get-rich-quick read. We want you to know that the tools are out there; you just need to learn how to use them, and there has never been a better time to be excited about the advantages of sitting in the chair you are in right now.

The tools are as common as any nail gun purchased at a hardware store. Sure, you can run right out and buy a nail gun, but a sane person would get some training on proper use prior to pointing and shooting that device for delivering metal projectiles–because if you bypass the training, you might just nail yourself to a wall.

We're not sure why so many people think having big box of tools and no training makes them master digital carpenters. Maybe it's the fact that in just a shade over ten years, the science of marketing has become what was thought to be science fiction only ten years before. The art of marketing changes at a much slower pace than the science, however. The art of building a solid relationship with people and a foundationally good product or service is more important today than it was ten years ago, but the art of building that relationship hasn't changed at all.

Art, as it happens, includes building a solid strategic framework in how you approach business. A solid strategic framework demands your undivided attention to understanding how each and every tool in the digital marketing tool box works.

Data is the tinder fueling digital marketing technology's wildfire growth rate. The consuming public has decided to voluntarily tell companies almost everything they could ever know about them, and marketers are learning how to use that knowledge. Big tech and big data's speed of advancement has outpaced the marketer's ability to truly harness it.

Digital marketing, social data consumption, and the nonexistence of any sort of barricade to keep anyone with an ad buck from accessing the data has catapulted marketing technology forward. Yet, small businesses still think their best marketing bet is a baseball cap with their logo on it. At the opposite end of the spectrum, medium-sized companies and emerging challenger brands have placed marketing disciplines into lone operating units or silos in order to better capitalize on the unique skill sets each discipline demands.

Search, display, e-mail, and analytics all require different skills to be done properly, but these tools must all work toward the same goal at all times—that's where marketing automation and finding the right tools are extremely helpful.

The biggest barrier to the success of the future Davids has nothing to do with technology, cloud-based engineering, or automation. It's the same thing that has plagued David since the dawn of time: self-defeat. We look at the size of the Goliath and think we have been beaten before we begin the fight. The sad, ironic problem with this age-old Achilles heel is that in today's marketing world, which is driven by the transparency the digital universe has thrust upon us, Goliath is dressing up in David camouflage. We live in a world where big brands have a disadvantage and launch "cottage" siblings to change the perception of their big brand status.

Examples of big brands buying boutique equity are everywhere, but you needn't look further than your kitchen. The packaged goods universe has become ground zero for the giant boutique. Being a big brand has never been more of a liability. If it weren't important to maintain boutique and independent status, it's doubtful the Coca Cola Company would have kept intact not only the Vitamin Water brand name but also its management team when it purchased the company in 2007.

Brand perception and storytelling are more important than ever (apparently) to people buying ice cream as well. Beloved brand Ben and Jerry's ice cream has been owned and operated by the Anglo-Dutch Unilever conglomerate since April 2000. Neither Ben nor Jerry have been involved in the day-to-day operations of the ice cream brand for well in excess of a decade; yet, the company maintains its small-town neighborhood, freethinking feel. In short, big company, small identity works.

Jostein Solheim took over the reins of Ben and Jerry's in 2010. Solheim was widely quoted as placing emphasis on the importance and role of a business based on values. A "values-based" business is a nice way of referring to a company as the venture of a storyteller and social activist. When Solheim was appointed head of all things Ben and Jerry, his quote was very telling: "Historically, this company has been and must continue to be a pioneer to continually challenge how business can be a force for good and address inequities inherent in global business."

What does the mandated independence of both the brand and the business in the Vitamin Water and Ben and Jerry's examples tell you? It's a very clear message that your boutique, challenger, or independent rebel status is something of value. The value of maintaining an independent small-town look, feel, and genuine nature is measurable. In other words, conglomerates are investing heavily in making themselves just like you. If they weren't, we might have seen "VitaCoke" make an appearance in 2007. That's what we call a gift-wrapped level playing field.

So let's recap what you learned in each of the chapters in *Taking Down Goliath*, starting with a few questions you absolutely must answer before putting this text down.

KNOWN DIGITAL MARKETING UNIVERSE

Can you get past the flavor-of-the-day syndrome?

Every day new technologies arrive on the scene. While they all claim to be earth-shattering, only some of them are, and only a small percentage of those become "need to haves." The digital marketing universe demands that every person practicing the art of an attempted human connection vet out the crappy also-ran technologies by letting those with a lot more money be the guinea pigs. To put it simply, you don't have the money to chase every new gadget. You need a sensible approach to evaluating new tools, technologies, and toys. It's OK to create annual plans and define long-term strategies as long as you keep the tactics (or the channels) flexible.

The days of making a quick buck by exploiting weaknesses in the connected marketing world have come to an end. And this is a good thing for you.

MEASUREMENT OVERDRIVE

Is obsessing over the details bad?

Analytics is the easiest place in the world to make very big mistakes over and over again. Using multiple measurement tools and resources is your insurance policy against stupid mistakes. Never mind the folks who can't prioritize learning about their KPIs; some of the earliest examples of online marketing measurement consisted of advertisers counting millions of dollars in revenue that didn't exist because the analytics weren't configured correctly. And it wasn't some ridiculously complex configuration, it was something easy like the wrong box was checked (ticked, if you're in the United Kingdom) and just as easily fixed. We hope that last scenario doesn't sound outlandish, because that sort of thing happens every day. No kidding, every day.

Later in the digital analytics evolution marketers added so many data points together they started drawing conclusions with terribly flawed lines of correlation. Remember, a correlation (or a digital connection) between two variables (or success criteria or audience behavioral details or things that people click on) doesn't mean the first variable caused the other variable to occur. Whether it's making very simple mistakes or really big ones, remember that a mathematical house of cards isn't going to help you build a sustainable business.

KNOW YOUR AUDIENCE

Who are these people, really?

There are no excuses left for not getting to know the people buying stuff from you. People want you to know things about them so you can learn how often they want you to contact them and what they want you to say to them. They have given you their blessing to learn about them. So what are you waiting for, an engraved invitation? Well, yes, you should have an invitation, and you can collect all kinds of information about what people do and where they do it. Just remember, you should always, always, always be careful with your customer's personal information. A little transparency and disclosure will go a long way toward helping you build a better relationship with your new, existing, and potential customers.

MESSAGING PERFECTION

What do you have to say about yourself?

Being genuine has never been more of an asset. Trying to hide anything has never been more of a liability. Read between the lines; everyone knows everything all the time. Act accordingly. The message of being genuine is the only one anyone wants to hear. It's the only one that's going to sustain your brand. As marketing automation becomes more sophisticated, so will the tools that will help you make the right decisions. Remember, each and every message has to be consistent, it has to be true, and it has to be 100 percent accurate. This is good news for you because having access to all these amazing tools makes it easier and cheaper to test a lot of different messaging elements. You should know how each message you communicate is received by your target audience.

E-MAIL AND YOU

Why are trying to talk to me?

E-mail is the first digital communications format that we could refer to as a utility. The same way electricity has other uses, its first priority is life-preserving heat and light. There are several types of utilities in the digital marketing world, but e-mail's first priority is necessary communication. E-mail is the result of an expressed indication of interest. Interests can be very narrow, or they can be very wide. Success depends on using the information you have on your potential customer base. You must learn when and why you should send someone an e-mail. They will interact if you get them on the right day at the right time with the right message. Days of the week and different hours during the day matter, and performance will vary by interest and category. You're going to have to figure out how to isolate your customer's preferences for receiving information. If you treat e-mail like a public trust that should always be handled delicately, you still won't win every time, but you'll get more than one chance to get it right.

RICHER MEDIA

Is there a wealth of interaction here?

I'm not sure about the interaction part, but look at it this way: you don't just decide you want to be a professional fighter and step into the ring with Apollo Creed. Since the first digital ad appeared back in early days of online marketing, people have lusted after ads and other communication formats that create a richer experience. The rich selling proposition is simple; it creates a more intense experience for the advertisers. The practical aspects of the evolution of rich formats include (but are not limited to) videos that roll automatically with no one watching, ads that pop up, creating an annoying experience for everyone on the Internet and videos that don't load at all where the primary message seems to be "buffering." We've often thought that creating a product called "buffering" would be total genius because we'd get tons of free air time through other people's ads or videos that never seem to load.

Here's a good rule of thumb: if the richer format creates an environment that will help you engage your audience, the experience is justified. If you are simply utilizing intense graphics and moving creative designs for the sake of doing so, you might be setting yourself up for a big fail. Know your formats and know your placements at all times.

SEARCH ADS

Can you match message and intent?

The find-and-replace of intent marketing should be the hero of digital. Search ads spawned from a desire to turn search engines into digital phone books. Every time online advertising has crashed, search ads came to the industry's rescue. Search ads have been the only stable growing and largely unchanged ad format in the industry. Other than labeling changing from "sponsored" to "ad" and back again, the search ad is essentially the same thing it was the day was introduced. Yet, it remains the stepchild of the business because it's simple and to the uninitiated it lacks creativity. While search ads may appear to lack creativity from a purely visual perspective, a proper search engine advertising initiative can serve to enhance your brand, enhance your positioning, capture interest, and help build credible perception of your online presence simply because you are present in search results.

Search ads can be the best performing ads in your online advertising toolbox, but you must remember to steer clear of simply looking at the last click. While the search ad might be your best performer from the perspective of direct attribution, you must understand that every other aspect of your committed online communications and advertising will have a direct impact on search.

CONTENT OPTIMIZATION

Can you be unbiased and overinform?

Search is another Internet utility that to some represents a public trust. For their part, many search site owners have worked hard to maintain this public trust because it makes good business sense. If you can't learn to invest heavily in something you have little or no control over, you'll never really understand search engine optimization. Once called natural or editorial listings because people thought that the integrity of search engine results couldn't be bought, search engine optimization can and will remain a fundamental aspect of digital marketing.

While search sites continue to change the rules on an almost daily or weekly basis, the same basic "I learned them in kindergarten" disciplines are as effective today as they were ten years ago. In spite of all the SEO mythology, from a technical perspective, the act of optimizing is largely transparent. Make sure your website can be "seen," and make sure to correct technical errors when they appear. Search sites will actually tell you when these errors appear and how to correct them.

Other rules in the search world should be plain as day. Don't build content farms. Don't try to game the system. Know the rules. Expect that changes will occur that will affect you and have a backup plan. As with other marketing disciplines, don't rely exclusively on editorial listings as your only marketing channel. Above all, don't take search algorithm changes personally; there's a good chance the search engine "isn't out to get you."

SOCIAL MEDIA

Can the universe's epicenter of bad behavior work for you?

Trying to market in a social environment is like trying to referee sixth-grade dodgeball. There are all kinds of people behaving in all kinds of ways on Facebook and other social channels. There is an enormous amount of data available for all marketers to consume and a growing network of technologies to control viewing. There are tools to tell you what to be and where to tell your story. There are tools that report back on interpretations of your creative on a large scale, and they are free as long as you keep buying ads.

A social ad is the most volatile of ad formats. These ads seem to change almost hourly. Rather than worry about keeping up with the changes, your main concern should be maintaining a genuine nature in your communications. If you want to be obsessed about something in social media marketing, be obsessed about staying relevant and keeping all forms of communication appropriate to each venue. Some social destinations react better to visual or graphic representations, and some react better to text or conversational aspects of communication. Make the right decisions based on how your audience chooses to interact with you and remember that social media are not one-way broadcast media.

MOBILITY AND MARKETING

Is 20?? the year of mobile?

Of course, it is. Every year mobile "arrives." Any combination of a series of events not necessarily connected can lead to that particular year being declared the year of mobile. Since 1997 every year has been the year of mobile. You can pretty much count on mobile being the technology of the year next year as well. Why does everyone want this year to be the year mobile arrives? It's simple, really; the advancements occurring in mobile technologies are far outpacing desktop technologies. And an app-centric environment seems easier to build and play in for developers than an environment centered on an operating system.

The most important thing to remember about mobile is that you have to remain flexible in this dynamic environment. The preferred method of engagement for your potential customers must be appropriate for the device that customers are consuming information on—that is, don't give me mobile ads intended for desktop consumption on my tablet. Don't think you can automatically "convert" all campaigns to mobile devices by hitting a button. It sounds pretty simple, right? See that it is simple for your audience, and you'll enjoy the rewards.

For the record and though it should go without saying, if you are ten chapters into this book, the authors aren't just waxing poetic about being David companies and leveling the playing field in a Goliath world. Writing *Taking Down Goliath* in no way contained any of the following ingredients:

- Checks from companies (other than the publisher)
- Corporate-sponsored vanity publishing
- Cushy jobs that allowed us to sit in a room and write while we collected a salary

Nope, *Taking Down Goliath* was good old-fashioned work for 20-hour days while trying to pay our rent, our employees, and our taxes. We practice what we preach.

There are one or two things we've learned from the world. Good things happen when you apply wisdom to knowledge. Good things happen when you level the playing field. Good things for business and good things for humanity. Sometimes, you have to lend the playing field a helping hand, that's what we hoped to accomplish with this book.

APPENDIX: WHAT'S A DAVID PROFILE?

One of the key discoveries we made in writing this book was that the Davids of advertising can come in a lot of forms. They are not just the little guys who have to compete with budgets and brands with a lot more spending power.

Throughout writing *Taking Down Goliath*, we thought of our friends, colleagues, brands we admired, and, more important, the people who help these challenger brands move forward.

We hope that *Taking Down Goliath* is something you can return to from time to time for a little bit of knowledge and perhaps some inspiration. In the pages following the main text of the book, we have included selected interviews with people from companies of all sizes. We tirelessly sought out people with genuine stories, a genuine nature, and an appreciation for the spirit of the book.

We have business owners, a manager of a Fortune 500 company, a luxury boutique brand commerce manager, and even a chief marketing officer. We intentionally varied the questions to help frame the difficult challenges these people face and perhaps help you in your quest to take down your own Goliath.

Your Goliath may be an internal challenge, it may be learning to work in a collaborative environment, or it may be facing of the challenge of coexisting with Goliath as one of our interviewees discovered. Amy Fletcher, founder of AE Fletcher Photography (after ditching her studio job) found big brands to be her clients. Or, as Fara Abramson tells us, she's not trying to keep up with big brands, she's just trying to give people something they can't get anywhere else.

Some of our interviews humbled us. Blake Rockwell, founder of Special Spectators, explained how focus can help you avoid chasing your tail (and maybe your competition) when he told us he never thinks about keeping up with big brands. Blake is said he's constantly focused on how Special Spectators can serve more kids. This leads us to our next point about our David profiles.

Who are these people, really? They are people we have met through industry events, hired to work for us, or in some cases they have hired us. They are champions in their own companies and in the industry. Consider Chris Moloney, chief marketing officer at Wells Fargo Advisors (a man who has taken down many a Goliath) and his advice on how to keep up with brands with a lot more spending power. He emphasizes having a clear and focused target audience and digital personas identified on your way to growth.

Why should you care? Because you are not alone. Being an entrepreneur can be lonely. But do you know what else can be really lonely? Working inside a big organization when your only responsibility is to touch a very narrow aspect of the marketing universe. Listen to Kelly DiNisco, digital marketing manager for Rachel Ashwell Shabby Chic Couture as she wonders most days if she's choosing the right marketing initiatives. Sound familiar?

We also can't wait for you to read about Erynn Petersen, who's an executive at Time, Inc., and runs a nonprofit or two. Erynn emphasizes the advantage that sincerity brings to you as a marketer. She also pointed out that customers and audiences have become interchangeable; any business with a customer has an audience. It sounds like Lubnah Salah, founder of House of Shakti, would agree with Erynn. Lubnah told us that her primary focus was making sure her story was communicated clearly.

Part of our focus in this book was checking hip trends in digital marketing against tried and true strategies. Over and over again, our interviewees emphasized the need of a strategic approach as you navigate making decisions on where to invest time and resources. As the digital marketing director for Aramark Parks & Destinations Marie Dumesnil explained to us, just because a social channel works (or perhaps appears to work) for a competitor, that's no reason to jump on a technology, particularly if you don't have the resources to put into it. Marie still emphasizes the value of a "good old-fashioned marketing plan."

The real crux of digital marketing lies in wading through the thousands of 99-cent e-books on "magic digital marketing." Jim Spanfeller, founder and CEO of Spanfeller Media Group, probably had some of the best advice for us. He said, "The amount of misguided and out-and-out criminal activity in digital marketing is crazy." Eugene Park from Bugaboo Mobility is focused on another, similar problem. Eugene advises that "there's also more clutter, hype, and misinformation than ever as well." Eugene says to do your homework.

Finally, we're happy to introduce you to Tameka Kee. Tameka is the founder of TJK Media, and her words about building something bigger than herself probably resonate with us best. She's looking to build a "viable business and not just an idea that I've convinced some of my friends (and some clients) to believe in." How true.

PROFILES OF DAVID: AMY FLETCHER

Meet Amy Fletcher, founder of A. E. Fletcher Photography. Amy saw a unique category of business rising around her unique skills. One of her core digital strategies includes taking advantage of the most popular format of sharing: photos. In the digital marketing information age, it's hard to hide anything, but after talking with Amy, we proved the old adage, "the camera doesn't lie."

1. What made you want to go out on your own?

Years ago, while working in a catalog photo studio, I started getting freelance work on the side, photographing executives for a financial trade magazine. Working for the magazine gave me direct contact with these executives, and sometimes their companies hired me directly to update their headshots for websites and marketing and PR purposes. After doing some research, I noticed that there was a hole in the market, and that maybe this could be my niche. I really liked photographing these executives, and there was definitely a growing need for *modern* headshots in the corporate world. The corporate work continued to grow, I ditched the studio job, and turned business headshots into a real business.

2. What makes you think you can keep up with big brands?

At this point, some big name companies are my clients, and that certainly helps me keep up with the big brands. Getting our foot in the door with one big company opened up many other doors, then they spread the word. As a small company, we can give them big-brand quality, but we make sure it's far more personalized. Our goal is to bring out the real personality of these executives and show that they are approachable, friendly, and, of course, professional. And that their companies are modern…and then they use these photos for their own digital marketing. At the risk of losing potential clients, I frequently talk them out of going with standard old-school gray or white background shots, and instead offer them something fresh and new. It's more important to do it right than to just do it for the money. It's a risk, but then the clients are pleased with the results, and they tell everyone they know (in person and online).

3. How did you frame your digital marketing strategy?

My business has always been based on word of mouth. When my clients love the work I've done for them, they spread the word simply by using those photos for their marketing purposes. Therefore, my digital marketing strategy is essentially sharing my work, sharing links to client websites, others commenting and sharing/tagging/commenting, and eventually my work becomes visible to new potential clients. Occasionally a client will share a new headshot on Facebook, tagging me, and it gets 100+ likes and comments, and I get a few new clients. And while we are still working on expanding our digital media reach (Facebook, Twitter, LinkedIn), I am already getting RFPs every week because someone outside of my network has seen my work through contacts on LinkedIn.

4. What is your biggest concern about the success of your business?

I am always concerned that business will dry up even though it's been growing more and more every year. Adding content to my website and building a good digital media strategy will continue to help combat dry spells and bring in new work (when in the past we'd just panic about filling up the calendar).

5. How do you use online marketing to separate you from the rest of the world?

Recently we have been having fun creating interesting (and sometimes silly) original content to put on the A. E. Fletcher Photography website, usually in the form of articles, blog posts, and slideshows, and then we share this on all forms of social media. The next step is to make sure people see it, especially on LinkedIn (where most of my corporate clients and potential clients are). When we share the link on LinkedIn and someone in my network likes it or, better yet, comments on it, a whole new world of people is then exposed to the articles. These posts show the personality of my company and often bring in new clients who hadn't previously seen my work.

6. Do you think online marketing lives up to all of its promises?

If done right, yes, online marketing lives up to its promises. What we've done so far has made a huge difference. I have faith that as we build the right online marketing strategy, my company will continue to grow and become an even stronger competitor.

7. When you think of throwing in the towel, what brings you back?

I genuinely love what I do. I think everyone deserves a great photo that shows who they are. (Stop using old photos just because you were thinner or had more hair, etc. Honesty is the best policy.) Some of my favorite moments, the ones that keep me in this, are when new clients tell me how excited they are about the shoot. Also, when people think they are not photogenic, it's fun to see that they are visibly surprised/pleased when I show them a sneak peek photo during the shoot. After they see that, they can relax and have fun. And then they share the final product on social media to show all their friends.

A current photo is honesty in marketing yourself or your company.

PROFILES OF DAVID: CHRIS MOLONEY

Meet Chris Moloney. Chris is the senior vice president and chief marketing officer at Wells Fargo Advisors, the retail investment arm of Wells Fargo. Before joining Wells Fargo, Chris was chief marketing officer at Experian and Scottrade. When Chris joined Scottrade, the firm was a little-known discount broker, and four years later had grown to be one of the largest online and branch-supported investment firms in the United States. During his time at Experian, Chris led the company through the acquisition of two significant online competitors to leapfrog fierce competition. Chris joined Wells Fargo Advisors when the brand was only two years old, and he helped lead the firm into the digital age to compete against fierce Goliaths with much bigger budgets and bigger brand awareness. Although he has worked for large organizations, Chris has always taken on the role of a David in an industry of Goliaths.

1. Are there times when you feel like you are on a digital marketing island?

I lead all marketing for my company, so I rarely feel isolated into just digital. Frankly, it feels like it takes 70 hours a week to adequately stay on top of digital and social trends, so as I manage both digital and traditional marketing as well as strategic marketing direction for the company, I miss spending more time in the digital arena.

That said, I've worked for a number of companies with little to no digital presence where I have felt I was a lonely voice pushing for change. Bigger companies have deep resources but are often outmaneuvered by smaller and more nimble companies. The trick is to think like a small company and try to stay sharp and think entrepreneurially. Complacency is the enemy.

In spite of how much we understand the ways in which digital and mobile behaviors are driving both consumer and business behaviors, so much business is still built around more traditional business trends. It can feel lonely when fighting for digital budget, and that's just as true in larger companies as it is in small ones.

2. What strategies do you use to keep up with bigger budget brands?

Many of our competitors outspend us in marketing by large amounts. Digital marketing can be a great equalizer when you can't afford to spend tens of millions on brand awareness through traditional methods. Having a clear and focused target audience and digital personas identified can allow you to find and follow your best prospects and thus contribute to the growth of the company in a tangible, measurable way.

For me, search marketing and retargeting are two ways to get close to your prospects and to deliver the right message at the right time and place. We also developed some unique and effective multivariate display ad testing that taught us a lot. The biggest breakthrough in digital that I have been a part of involved dynamic real-time content in digital ads that met what people were searching for at that instant. That one was fun because I got deeply involved in filing a patent for digital media technology.

Digital ad testing can be a long and complex process, and it can feel very different for a marketing leader who is more comfortable focusing on areas such as brand and long-term results, but it can be rewarding to explore this path fully and know when you need to pull back and simplify.

3. How did you frame your digital marketing strategy?

For me, strategy generally falls into two camps: either bottom-up or top-down. For an overall digital strategy, I aim to blend both. I know a number of highly technical digital gurus. I've spent a lot of time digging into the technical opportunities that exist in the digital space, which involves getting into the weeds and exploring day-to-day digital details. As a CMO though, I find it hard to find that time, but it's still worth it.

The advantage of a bottom-up or digital-centric strategy is that you can really take advantage of what makes digital and mobile marketing unique. Far too many companies still think of TV or mass media first. It's important to consider thinking of digital first when developing targeting and messaging. The risk of this bottom-up strategy, however, is that you may do something really technically cool—but you overengineer it or you fail to tie it to the bigger marketing strategy and mission of the company. So, it's important to seek a balance here.

As for the top-down, I think it's important to evaluate the broad and big-picture needs of the company before diving into digital solutions. Often, the connection of a company to its customers has an important emotional aspect to it. When diving headlong into digital advertising tactics, often that emotional value is lost. Some CEOs would say "spend all your money on Google search" if measuring ROI was the only objective. But advertising is an art and a science. Digital has raised the bar on how much of this can be scientific, but there's still quite a bit of art out there in marketing. Top-down strategy often includes that emotional and longer-term thinking that is essential to good marketing.

4. What is your biggest concern about the success of your line of business?

I worry most about investing in the right digital and mobile innovations. How do you divide a budget between mobile app technology and responsive web design? These choices are important and can be costly. It's not just about dollars of investment either; it's about how much time and resources you give to the next generation of digital.

Placing a bet on the right digital investments can keep you up at night. CMOs are not the "in the weeds" experts. It's essential to surround yourself with bold digital thinkers who challenge you and live it every day. I think CMOs are like good baseball coaches: They never hit or catch, but they get their best players on the field to win. I talk about digital with people smarter than me every day, and I hope just enough rubs off on me that I can place some good bets once in a while.

5. How do you use online marketing to separate you from the rest of the world?

One key to digital is having the right message at the right time in the right place. Offering me investment news where and when I am reading movie reviews is bad placement.

Two more keys to digital are making digital personal and local. Too often, digital strategies lack an emotional element, and they are too tactical or scientific. When you can use the science of online marketing to make an emotional connection, you have hit gold! The second tip is local. Digital allows you to deliver the right message to someone in the right place more than ever, and with the proliferation of smartphones, consumers expect to have access to information and services on the go. This capability is key to digital, and this trend will continue to evolve rapidly. I have had four or five recent moments of delight when a digital solution caught me at just the right time of need or want. This ability to be both local and personal is the "diamond" of the industry, and few have come close to capturing it so far.

6. Do you think online marketing lives up to all of its promises?

No. There is so much absurd hype around useless trends that causes marketers to too often waste a lot of time chasing shiny objects. We all say we need to avoid the next bright shiny object, but we all fall for it.

The potential for digital and online marketing is immense. Companies that can leverage the ability to be personal and relevant, without being creepy, can do amazing things.

7. When you think of throwing in the towel, what brings you back?

Digital marketing happy hours! No, seriously, I think when you've had some pretty cool successes with digital marketing, you can get hooked. It's such a fun and fast-paced industry that you just know the next big thing (or many little things) is out there waiting to be captured. I guess it's like your golf game. The bad shots frustrate the heck out of you, but a handful of awesome moments make you want to go back and try it again.

Lastly, I think there's an exciting value in being able to connect some of these successes with larger strategic goals and share these with folks newer to the business or young marketers. Helping to get them fired up about making these connections is pretty exciting. When the digital team members see the impact they are having on the business—they are the most fun and exciting group to be around. Just avoid being the one holding the tab at the end of a happy hour where you celebrate the "win."

PROFILES OF DAVID: FARA ABRAMSON

Meet Fara Abramson, the founder of Presence of Piermont, a boutique store located in an upstate New York hamlet. Fara is in our opinion the quintessential perseverant dreamer. Her way of taking down Goliath in the digital world includes maintaining personal relationships with her customers through social media and direct one-on-one communication channels.

1) What made you want to go out on your own?

I was in graduate school getting a master's degree in social work, and I didn't really like it. So I called my mother and told her that I didn't want to do this anymore and instead I wanted to open a store, and we started talking about what to put in the store, and my mother thought it should be the kinds of stuff I like to buy. And that's pretty much how we set it up together.

It really wasn't a big plan or dream for me. Instead it just came to me. I said it out loud, and it happened! I don't recommend this approach. I think it might make more sense to have a plan and actually work in the field first before starting a store!

But I was lucky that my mother could help me to afford all the mistakes that we made, and we've survived now for a long time.

2) What makes you think that you can keep up with the big brands?

I'm not trying to keep up with the big brands, and I don't think I can. Instead, I try to offer my customers things that they can't buy anywhere else. In truth, when I make buys, I sometimes ask who else they are selling to. If it's a big vendor, then I know the item won't be unique, and I generally won't buy it.

3) How do you frame your digital marketing strategy?

I have a little planning and a little off-the-cuff, "whim-of-the-day" marketing. For example, my Facebook posts are really whim of the day, but my e-mails are much better planned. I sometimes use a calendar to help me market around calendar events. Since I sell gifts, I learn about ways to sell to specific events or holidays.

For my e-mails I'm reaching about 1,200 people, but this is a list I built. These are all opt-ins who have given me full permission to contact them.

4) What is your biggest concern about the success of your business?

My location. My store is well placed, but the town is changing. Retail businesses are closing and being replaced mostly with restaurants, which makes it harder to have Piermont stand out as a place to go shopping. But I have found that my e-mail campaigns really do end up driving traffic to the store. Every so often I send out coupons in the e-mails and find that a lot of people show up at the store with coupons in hand. People actually come in and tell me that they look forward to my e-mails!

5) How are you using digital marketing to separate Presence from your competitors?

Well, I keep a close eye on my social media fan numbers. Not the amount of people I have as a fan base but my percentage of people talking about my store. And I try really hard not to make my posts about sales, because not everything is about sales, but instead the personality of the products I sell and how my fan base reacts to them. I like to post things that are fun and often things that have absolutely nothing to do with my store! Those are the things I get the most response on, but it keeps Presence fresh in the customers' mind.

6) Do you feel that online marketing lives up to the hype and promise that vendors often give to it?

Yes, I do. Without it, marketing would be so much harder. I have people who come into the store because of things I posted on Facebook that morning.

7) When you have one of those days where you wake up and ask yourself "why am I doing this?" what is it that gets you out of bed and keeps you going?

Sometimes if I'm venting to a close friend, the friend will remind me that I do the same thing every year at the same time. Especially during our slow season. But I've discovered that if I click on my point-of-sale program and compare the previous year's numbers, I'm always surprised to find that I'm doing better than I was back then. I sometimes need that reminder.

PROFILES OF DAVID: KELLY DINISCO

Meet Kelly DiNisco, digital marketing manager for Rachel Ashwell Shabby Chic Couture. Kelly is living proof that marketing managers need not command seven- or eight-figure budgets to compete in the modern digital marketing ecosystem. We first met Kelly when she was director of e-commerce at another amazing brand, Linea Pelle, and she's an expert at accomplishing a lot with limited resources. Her digital strategic core includes always keeping an eye on what's coming next and maintaining her commitment to brand.

1. Are there times when you feel like you are on a digital marketing island?

Yes, most days I feel this way. There is so much opportunity to increase your presence online, and the thought is "Am I choosing the right marketing initiatives," "Would this work better for the brand," and the never-ending "What is everyone else doing." It is so all-encompassing and a bit overwhelming because of that never-ending opportunity.

2. What strategies do you use to keep up with bigger budget brands?

I figure out what my budget is and how I can best use that to compete. Instead of putting a little bit everywhere, I figure out which digital marketing platform would bring new customers and keep existing customers excited and go full force that way. It is my philosophy to do one thing 100 percent rather than a bunch of things 10 percent. I always understand that I am never going to compete with Amazon, but look at brands that are close enough so that I can steal a customer.

3. How did you frame your digital marketing strategy?

I have a marketing calendar that I try to plan out loosely for the next six months to a year and firmly for three months at a time. I am always aware that things will change a bit, but if I can stay as true to it as possible, I am always more successful. If I plan properly, I am able to estimate where I am going to spend my budget, which usually results in better reaction from customers and in sales.

4. What is your biggest concern about the success of your line of business?

My concerns change from minute to minute. Is my e-commerce platform the best it can be, is the product still resonating with customers, how can I keep my current customers interested while gaining new customers—that's what I think about. In truth, my biggest concern is that I am always aware of what I should be doing next for the brand. It's a lot to keep up with.

5. How do you use online marketing to separate you from the rest of the world?

Currently, I work for a brand that is based around the ideas and designs of the founder. She is the inspiration and the draw even more so than the product. I try to always remember that when I am marketing the company. It actually makes my job a little easier. In the past I have had to analyze how to make the product different from everything else that is out there.

6. Do you think online marketing lives up to all of its promises?

Sometimes. The bottom line is you need to spend money to gain brand awareness, you can't sit back and do nothing. The challenge is picking the right marketing strategy for your brand. Would choosing a platform geared toward young people when I have older consumers make sense? No, it wouldn't but what if the goal was to grow my customer base to reach a younger demographic, then that idea would change. In my experience I also believe that just throwing money at a strategy doesn't work either. You must stay on top of it. Even if it's an Ad Word program, those terms should always be monitored. If you aren't paying attention to your strategy and you are not seeing results, you can only blame yourself.

6. When you think of throwing in the towel, what brings you back?

I realize that I enjoy what I do. I am the ultimate consumer so looking at it from the marketer perspective is easy for me.

PROFILES OF DAVID: ERYNN PETERSEN

Meet Erynn Petersen. When we think of Erynn, we think of a person who is the real deal. She's been there, she's done that, and there aren't many stones she hasn't turned over in her career. Erynn has held senior management positions at world-renowned brands and helped build nonprofit organizations. In addition to having been an executive at Time, Inc., and Microsoft, Erynn is executive director at Outercurve foundation and a board member at Girl Develop It and Station082, leading the charge to increase the number of people pursuing careers in engineering.

1. What made you go out on your own?

When you work for a big company, you get used to big-company infrastructure. This is especially true if you're an exec: you get used to being away from the details, and you forget what it's like to be hands-on. Even if you are convinced that you know what goes on in the trenches, you get used to working through a level of abstraction between you and the details, you and the little problems that sap energy from a business, and between you and your customers. I try to take a sabbatical about every five years, and when I'm on sabbatical I take on projects that ground me in the basics of my customers or audience. When I was younger, people didn't get this, but I've found over the long arc of my career that it's been really effective. Now I'm back in a big company, but the lessons from the last year really stick with me. I still have my company on the side, and I'm looking for someone to run it.

2. What makes you think you can keep up with the big brands?

We're in an era where we are moving away from a culture that values irony to a culture that values sincerity, and we're also moving from a culture where you can manage the story behind your brand (what your story is, the channels in which it appears, how your story is told) to an era where customers and audiences know the real story with your brand. Customers and audiences have become interchangeable; any business with a customer has an audience. Your customers are hearing your story from you on social media channels, your customers are hearing your story from the point of view of other customers, and your customers are telling their version of your story.

Big companies find both of these changes to be discomfiting. They have become accustomed to managing their image with consistent messaging that they have purchased and control. They are used to casting their message ironically, especially if their brand is (or purports to be) values-based in how they connect to customers.

If you are a small business, you are used to this new dynamic: you can't control what your neighbors say about you, for example, so if you plan to be around for a while you take good care of your customers, and you're a good citizen. You donate goods for school raffles, you're nice to people when you run into them at the grocery store. You want everyone to think well of you, and you are acutely aware that treating someone badly is going to result in a lost customer and gossip at the Saturday morning soccer game. You're fighting for every customer, and you can't afford to lose them. So if you're having a bad day and still need to grocery shop, you go to the store one town over. You have to live and demonstrate personally and commercially the values you espouse.

Big companies are used to being able to manage the discourse around mistakes. They have been able to distance themselves from mistakes made by employees and put an ironic cast on errors made when their espoused values don't align with their actions or outcomes. A classic example is Jack in the Box (I have been and remain a Jack in the Box fan; I love the shakes and the tacos at Jack in the Box). They had a core market of kids and families, and when they had the E. coli incident in the early 90s, many people thought they were toast. But then they turned around and built an entirely new brand identity that turned inside out what clowns, burgers, and American fast food was all about. It was a brilliant repackaging of a brand that could not have been accomplished as easily using social media, and probably couldn't have been done at all if they hadn't been able to buy giant swaths of TV time.

The beauty of the Jack in the Box campaign is that it was ironic but established the Jack as a person (if you can call a person with a giant fake head a person) and that person himself, while ironic, has a deep sense of integrity. This sense of integrity informs the persona, and was used infamously to turn on its head the world shift to digital media by dismissing the social media strategist in the hashtag commercial.

And here is where we come full circle: a small business just wouldn't have a social media strategist on hand to "curate the brand" to "think outside the box" and "align social to further the mission of our entire web presence" (which are all direct quotes from a social media strategist angry about the Jack in the Box hashtag commercial in a post defending the profession). A small business talks to its customers directly: on Facebook, on Twitter, in the vegetable aisle at the grocery store.

In my world as a small business owner, I can have effective one-on-one conversations with my customers. I hear right way if my team has delivered a good experience or a bad experience. And in my corporate job I am grounded in an understanding that I am not "managing my conversation with my audience" and trying to get them "to click" and "convert"; I instead focus on building real experiences that solve real problems for real people and then sit back and let them say what they will about having their personal experiences with our brands.

3. How did you frame your digital marketing strategy?

(a) As manager in a small business, my digital marketing strategy is about making sure that customers know the basics about us: when we are open, how much we cost, what we do. This is much harder than it sounds. Fifteen years ago, I could have bought an ad in the paper and taken advantage of the foot traffic in my downtown small-town location. Today, there is no foot traffic in my downtown location, and buying an ad in the paper is expensive, and no one sees it.

(b) For the last year we really struggled with both running the business and marketing the business. Marketing a small business takes time, and the landscape for reaching an audience is fractured. It was our first year open, and just trying to figure out how to juggle the little things (making sure staff shows up, taking care of the toilet when it overflows, dealing with circuit breakers built in 1928 before anyone anticipated having a million electronics in a small retail space). One of our goals for this year is to put resources into our digital marketing. We've hired a social media person and are hiring a project manager to track all of the deadlines and collateral associated with our efforts. We get tons of pictures of our customers, for example, but we have been weak on putting them up and tracking their effectiveness. We haven't tracked which campaigns have worked well and which audiences we've connected with and why. This year we're putting about 25 percent of our payroll expenses into this effort.

(c) The last year wasn't completely wasted; we've listened to how our customers tell our story, and we're basing our efforts on that story. We thought, for example, that the audience for our Xbox business was teenagers; it turns out that it's middle schoolers and their moms. So now we're shifting our marketing to Facebook and Pinterest to reach moms and a little bit on Twitter. We're also going to be shifting to using RebelMouse to manage our site and our social media presence. We've tested that this year, and it's worked very well for us.

4. What is your biggest concern about the success of your business?

Getting customers through the door. Getting our number of visitors up, getting our rate of return visitors up, and getting our revenue per visit up. This is what everyone worries about as a small business!

5. How do you use online marketing to separate you from the rest of the world?

We are still at a point where we're telling our story. No one knows what an Xbox café is! For the first six months, people were convinced that teens would start coming in and getting stoned in our bathroom. After a year parents believe that we are a well-lit, safe place for kids to come, hang out, eat snacks, and play. A year of showing pictures of kids having fun and comments from parents has gone a long way for us.

6. Do you think online marketing lives up to all its promises?

There's still so much to do, especially for small local businesses. It's hard to reach your audience. Audiences are so fragmented. Facebook is a good way to reach your audience, but the data that comes back about the performance of your campaign changes all the time, and there's so little data about how much you are really paying to reach your audience. It was obvious when they changed the algorithms last fall that surfaced your content more effectively in feeds if you were paying for both placement and targeted campaigns, but there was so little transparency about it that it was a total pain in the ass. That experience alone, if I had less understanding of the industry, might have driven me back to newspapers out of desperation.

7. When you think about throwing in the towel what brings you back?

Probably the fact that my kids, my sister, and one of my best friends work for me! I'm kind of kidding about that. Here is what brings me back: we'd been open about a month and there was a kid who worked for me. He had come in to hang out on his off day, and I was sitting on a couch with him, and he turned around and said to me "Before this was here, I had nowhere to go." I think about him all the time. There was a session at SXSW where an investor from Maveron said that he invests in start-ups where, if the start-up closed down, people would really miss it. I think about my employees and my customers. I have kids who come in every day, rain or shine. They have their favorite couches, and they have a little community that they've built up. So when the business in struggling, I dig deep to figure out how to make it work and how to make it scale. We'll get there.

PROFILES OF DAVID: BLAKE ROCKWELL

Meet Blake Rockwell, founder and executive director of the nonprofit organization Special Spectators. Blake is a believer. In just a shade over a decade, Blake has built Special Spectators into an organization that has served 7,300 seriously ill kids and their families, 50 hospitals, and 45 schools, on campuses nationwide. In 2014, the organization will greatly expand the number of kids served and colleges involved as well as venture fully into professional sports. The digital marketing world has created some unique opportunities for Special Spectators, but it also serves to remind us of the intense challenges facing a small start-up. Even one with the best intentions in the world.

1. What made you want to go out on your own?

I created Special Spectators out of a need—my own and that of the seriously ill kids I met while volunteering.

The original idea for Special Spectators hatched while I volunteered at Children's Memorial Hospital (now Ann and Robert H. Lurie Children's Hospital of Chicago) more than 20 years ago.

As a sports fan, I quickly learned that many of the incredible patients I met shared my passion for sports. I had assumed sports wouldn't necessarily be of interest to most of these kids who were not well enough to participate. But to my delight the passion was definitely there. I was surprised to discover, however, that very few of these kids had ever attended a game of any kind. Most of their exposure to sports was watching it on television or through video games. I began to think how great it would be to *someday* host a group of kids at a game and provide a full day of fun and excitement—bringing joy to whole families weighed down by their children's illnesses. As someone who grew up in a household where an older brother had died just eight months before I was born, I understood this weight and knew the value of uncomplicated fun, such as taking a trip or going on an adventure together. Something we did a lot of when I was growing up.

Well, that "someday" I imagined arrived on September 11, 2001. By this time, I had moved to New York and was focused on my investment management career. On this day, two colleagues, one who had served as my interim boss while my full-time boss was on medical leave, were killed in the 9/11 attacks on the World Trade Center.

A couple of weeks later, a friend from Chicago, a nonsmoker in her early thirties died from lung cancer. I began to examine my life and what I was doing with it. I recalled this idea from my experience as a volunteer and decided to create Special Spectators.

2. What makes you think you can keep up with big brands?

I'm not sure if this is wise or foolish, but I never think about keeping up with big brands. I'm constantly focused on how we can serve more seriously ill kids, what steps are needed to do it better, and how we'll raise money to meet these goals.

3. How did you frame your digital marketing strategy?

Well, truthfully, this is a strategy still in the making. From the beginning, I've had an operating plan in place for event execution and the basic model of what we do, and a longer-term financial plan as well. Originally, we relied a lot on fairly basic PR and community relations. Over time, I established our web presence and some standard social media implementation. But as I've built out my team of marketing and business advisors, a broader strategy has started to take shape. As I said, we always look at our objective of serving more seriously ill kids first. But that objective has gotten more specific: more seriously ill kids, more seasons of the year, all year long. So, the goal is exponential. We'd like to serve as many kids, in as many communities, as we can, 365 days a year. To that end, we are shoring up our digital platforms, trying to do a better job of working across channels: website, Facebook, Twitter, and now mobile. And we tend to things like SEO, digital versions of PR, and some other stuff. I expect that as our strategy gets crystal clear and our execution broadens to where it needs to be, we'll be able to fill in more of the missing pieces. Plus, and this is very hard on a shoestring, we've taken care to put some basic analytics in place, tracking and measuring everything we do, so that we can learn from it, do more of what's working and drop what's not helping us toward our goals.

4. What is your biggest concern about the success of your business?

As we grow, become more popular, and host more game day events, my biggest concern is having the resources to do it all—time, money, and great people. Actually, speaking of digital marketing, one of the nuts we are still trying to crack is the online fundraising tactic.

5. How do you use online marketing to separate you from the rest of the world?

This also is still very much a work in progress. One of the new things we have introduced is a mobile/social component. We've integrated a mobile moment into most of our game day experiences to help build community through engaging fans, to engage with the kids, to send words of encouragement, and the like. This is unique. And we're going to be trying some new things with this next college football season.

6. Do you think online marketing lives up to all of its promises?

It can and should, assuming you have the resources to complete the picture. What does that mean? Well, it means you have to have the ability to develop and build the right digital platforms for your business or organization, the resources to produce and execute good creative, which includes doing something truly powerful with all your great video and photos (like we have), and of course, access to the right measurement and analytics tools. I do think—as with the online fundraising tools—there's a lot of hype in some areas, and these options are not broadly delivering on their potential for the communities and organizations they could serve.

7. When you think of throwing in the towel, what brings you back?

As someone who runs a nonprofit with no paid staff during my free time and relies on a national network of dedicated volunteers, I sometimes think of throwing in the towel. But then I recall the children's smiles and laughter, their stories shared by their parents, the thank-yous and hugs. Literally thousands of joyful family images run through my mind and my memory. How could I possibly give that up?

PROFILES OF DAVID: MARIE DUMESNIL

Meet Marie Dumesnil. Marie is a digital marketing director for a Fortune 500 brand, Aramark Parks & Destination's lodges and resorts in the United States. Prior to joining Aramark, Marie spent several years at Hilton Worldwide, where she played a key role for the Hilton family of brands. While at Hilton, she helped establish the first centralized content management process for the Hilton brands. She has received a variety of honors for her digital marketing achievements, including a Platinum Adrian Award from the Hotel Sales and Marketing Association International (HSMAI) and the Web Marketing Association Travel Standard of Excellence Award.

Marie is a long way from her birthplace in Paris, France, and her role is a slight departure from the big budget world, but her digital marketing strategy remains centered on enhancing and the customer's experience through online, mobile, and social platforms.

1. Are there times when you feel like you are on a digital marketing island?

Not anymore. I remember explaining my job 12 years ago when I was buying keywords on GoTo, and no one knew what I was talking about. I have now spent over 10 years in the hospitality and travel industry, and the majority of our marketing relies on digital, social, and mobile strategy. Everyone in the company, from the CEO to the operators at our lodges know that digital marketing is vital to our business, and that over 80 percent of our customers find us online. This doesn't mean that my budget and resources are unlimited, and I often have to make the case for increased spend in certain digital areas, especially new ones that have not yet proven they could deliver an ROI.

2. What strategies do you use to keep up with bigger budget brands?

In my current position, the larger competitors are also distributors (online travel agencies). In general, they have much larger marketing budgets and end up competing with us especially in paid search. This leads to bookings for us, but we have to pay a commission. To keep up with this competition, we spend our paid search media budget wisely, only investing in our top markets (geo-targeting). We also market heavily to our database via e-mail, which tends to keep costs under control and yields a high ROI.

3. How did you frame your digital marketing strategy?

I threw away the frame a long time ago. By definition, a digital marketing strategy should remain extremely flexible. I still rely on sound business practices, though, as these apply to any marketing strategy.

4. What is your biggest concern about the success of your line of business?

The need to adapt to a marketing and distribution landscape that changes at lightning speed. The travel and hospitality industry relies very heavily on digital marketing for advertising and revenue, and the rules keep changing: one day you need to focus your search strategy (both paid and organic) on keywords, the next day keywords are no longer provided by Google, and your new focus needs to be content. These rules are changing for everyone, but larger organizations are sometimes better equipped with contingency budgets and trained personnel. This ever-changing landscape also makes it sometimes challenging to get buy-in from senior leadership when your digital road map evolves on a constant basis.

5. How do you use online marketing to separate you from the rest of the world?

By always testing new things. When a new feature becomes available through search or social, we'll dedicate a small budget to it and start testing. An example would be Facebook Custom Audiences, which we're matching against our own CRM database. The key is that we're only testing on a small scale first, then expanding if we're seeing success. We're not always jumping on the latest craze and are very careful with having a sound and sustainable digital strategy in place.

6. Do you think online marketing lives up to all of its promises?

It definitely brings in the traffic and revenue. It allows us to measure ROI for every new campaign we launch, and it also allows us to know our audiences like never before. However, not every new online marketing tactic is a success. The fact that Twitter or Pinterest or Instagram works for your competitor doesn't mean you should automatically have a presence if your audience is not there or you don't have the resources to manage it. You still need to rely on a good old marketing plan to make things work.

7. When you think of throwing in the towel, what brings you back?

I just love what I do. I feel lucky and privileged to have been able to witness the early days and incredible rise of digital marketing. It is exciting to have known Google or Facebook as start-ups in their infancy and see what huge, global brands they've become. And even though this industry is now extremely complex, I still get a kick out of simple things, like helping a friend with a small business launch their local AdWords campaign and getting their first referrals from the web.

PROFILES OF DAVID: LUBNA SALAH

Meet Lubna Salah, founder of House of Shakti. To say that Lubnah has digital marketing chops would be vastly understating her abilities. We first came across Lubnah over ten years ago when she was managing multimillion dollar advertising budgets for a variety of brands. Prior to launching her packaged goods e-commerce brand, House of Shakti, she gained experience in almost every aspect of digital marketing. Today, House of Shakti has a large following with customers in over 14 countries. When we approached Lubna for an interview, her main concern was helping other people overcome the challenges she faced when creating, launching, and funding her business. How's that for selfless? Lubna was just the kind of David we thought deserved her own page in our book.

1. What made you want to go out on your own?

I wanted to prove to myself that I could do it. I wanted to give something back to the world as well. Looking back on my start, I reached a point where I felt like I needed a change and that I had hit a glass ceiling. I wasn't really learning or building anymore so the reward wasn't there. There is also the perception that those of us not solely motivated by material wealth seem to be categorized as crazy. I set out to make a change and build something. My detractors often asked me why I would create my own brand instead of buying cheap product and mark it up. To me, that would be insane, but the business people I know thought I was nuts for trying to create a brand, not market a commodity.

2. What makes you think you can keep up with big brands?

I don't, and it wasn't about competing with big brands. When I started out, I didn't view big brands as my competition. My competition in the fashion category seemed to be the dominant retail channel. I am an optimist, but a lot of success can be likened to a lottery, and you have to realize you aren't always going to win. I went from being alone in my business to suddenly being very popular. I also found that once I achieved a level of success in digital, everyone wanted to know how I was doing it. When I began to engage people through social channels (my primary sales channel), I knew I was on to something in creating a personal experience that a big brand couldn't possibly create at my level. People told me what they thought of my product and passed along creative and constructive advice. That's when I knew I had something unique.

3. How did you frame your digital marketing strategy?

I used my experience in digital marketing, which gave me an edge over my competition. The lesson is not in having an edge, but knowing what edge you can use to your benefit. My strategy included making sure my website represented me well. I tried everything at first. I went to multiple sales channels like "commerce in a box" solutions, but I found them more concerned about their own traffic and focused on building their own brands. I got my products listed in multiple commerce engines, meaning websites that charge you a fee for listing your products. The next challenge was making sure I was visible, recognizing that I would never beat the commerce listing engines in getting on the search results pages. Once I had positioning, it was time to create demand, and for that I went to social channels. When you have a jewelry brand, building the story around the brand is just as important as the quality of the product. Facebook dominates the rest of my social channels, and while I enjoy the interaction, no business should have a single point of failure. At the core of my strategy for approaching the medium and creating demand was making sure my business wasn't totally reliant on one communications channel. I had to make sure that my relationship with my customers was my own, not a social media website's or that of the commerce engine.

4. What is your biggest concern about the success of your business?

I don't want to be reliant upon one resource (or traffic source) for customers. Facebook is a great social platform, but it makes you reliant upon them for success. My biggest concern is the unknown. Technology is advancing at an alarming rate. There are tools available to me for managing a presence through social channels that didn't exist a year or two years ago. I have to be realistic about how much time, energy, and money I can allocate to selecting the right tools, hiring the right people. I maintain flexibility in how I approach each channel and the ability to change quickly and "pivot" in my business focus and resource allocation.

5. How do you use online marketing to separate you from the rest of the world?

My primary focus was making sure my story was heard. The power of my product is my story. There were two core areas of focus, reach and expression. In terms of reach, I could see the ripple effect of the information and the story I was telling. My social analytics told me what messages were not just resonating with the connected social channel, but what was really important to my customers. Businesses that only pay attention to popularity without separating what's important to their customers won't stand out from the crowd. I learn a great deal by analyzing social insights, and that helps me guide my focus on expression. My expression lies in my ability to tell a story, and aligning my interests and passions with what's important to my customers is core to setting my business apart. I would describe my expression through social channels as heavily curated—meaning I spend a lot of time cultivating relationships through storytelling—and that's a labor of love.

6. Do you think online marketing lives up to all of its promises?

Yes and no. The law of diminishing returns is pretty nowhere more prevalent than in the online world. What is the promise of online marketing? Easy money and untold wealth? I think the fantasy has caught up with reality: there are no shortcuts, and there is no substitute for having a sound strategic approach from the beginning. Simply following the guide provided by the company selling you ads will only tell you how to create an ad. Creating an ad is only part of the journey, and it's important to remember that the company selling you ads and how-to guides is motivated by selling you ads, not by building your business. Fundamentally, your product, pricing, and viability have to be your concern. Buying ads and signing up for so-called tools only serve to slow you down if you haven't thought through your business and communications strategy.

7. When you think of throwing in the towel, what brings you back?

The same motivation for building the business is the one that keeps me going. You face a lot of obstacles and roadblocks in growing a business, but I try to be a role model for women and my sisters by continuing to stand tall.

PROFILES OF DAVID: JIM SPANFELLER

Meet Jim Spanfeller. Jim is known throughout the world as an innovator in the digital marketing world. He's been the CEO of Forbes.com and volunteered his time for many years with one of the digital marketing industry's guiding standards organizations, the Interactive Advertising Bureau. With so many big names behind him, what is Jim doing in our book? In early

2011, Jim launched Spanfeller Media Group with premium content websites, *The Daily Meal* and later *The Active Times*. Jim faces an uphill battle in competing with much larger, more established brands in the digital content consumption ecosystem, and we think he'll be able to take down a Goliath or two.

1. What made you want to go out on your own?

I saw a huge opportunity in the market as analogue media companies consistently missed the fundamental changes being brought to bear by digital platforms. It also occurred to me that while I had been very successful creating lots of value for other folks, I had never really done it (other than a salary) for my family and me. Seemed like a good opportunity to give it a whirl.

2. What makes you think you can keep up with big brands?

In many ways it was the big brands that showed me this opportunity—not intentionally, of course. Just the same, their inability to understand the fundamental changes taking place was a huge catalyst for our efforts. Think about the change from plays to movies. The first movies were films of plays, simply porting one type of content into a new medium. In hindsight this is always the way legacy media acts around new advancements. It was not until someone realized that the camera could be moved that modern cinema was born. We are in a similar scenario now with digital. Derivative executions of porting analogue content solutions to digital platforms are nice but not nearly as compelling as they could be. In this light, having a big brand that is rooted in the past might not be as powerful as one would think.

3. How did you frame your digital marketing strategy?

From the ground up. Thinking what was possible, what was expected now compared to what has come before.

4. What is your biggest concern about the success of your business?

Like most start-ups, we are trying to do a lot with a little. I have not a doubt in the world that our strategies are on target, I just worry if we have the runway (read capital) to scale as quickly as the opportunity allows.

5. How do you use online marketing to separate you from the rest of the world?

By being different. By trying to recreate storytelling and journalism for a digital ecosystem.

6. Do you think online marketing lives up to all of its promises?

Not yet—but it will, without doubt. The issues now are twofold. First, we still have a lot to learn about how people respond to digital platforms and fundamentally what can really be done with them. Second, and way more depressing, because so much of digital is still dramatically misunderstood, there are a lot of bad actors. The amount of misguided and out-and-out criminal activity in digital marketing is crazy. We need to work hard to fix these issues before digital will be able to truly realize its full potential.

7. When you think of throwing in the towel, what brings you back?

I just think about how big the opportunity truly is and how stupid I would feel if I took a seat on the sidelines and watched others get there without me.

PROFILES OF DAVID: TAMEKA KEE

Meet Tameka Kee. Tameka is founder of TJK Media, a consultancy she launched after working for a variety of large companies. In addition to copywriting, ghostwriting, and content strategy, TJK produces events, video series, and lifestyle content for the always-on digital marketing professional. TJK Media works with partners such as Upstream Group, AdColony, and the Rubicon Project to create unique, delicious, and intriguing experiences across a variety of platforms. Tameka represents the best of driving factors for a lot of entrepreneurs; in addition striving to build a better product and service, she goes out of her way to work with the right kind people. Topping her list of things to accomplish is building something bigger than herself. We think she can do it.

1. What made you want to go out on your own?

From a practical standpoint, I'd reached a crossroads in my life and realized that traveling for an extended period of time was the next step for me. And then I realized that only way I'd be able to live abroad while sustaining the standard of living I'd become accustomed to here was to work for myself.

From a more esoteric standpoint, I wanted to do the kinds of work that I wanted to do and only work with the kinds of people that I wanted to work with. I know that sounds cliché, but it's more about the energy and drive of the people I like working with. I'm a "can-do, let's get it done quickly and effectively" person. I'm not a "this is the way it's always been done so we need to do it like this" person. Launching my own company was a way to ensure that I'd surround myself with collaborators and partners and clients that were just as driven and capable.

I also realized that I could earn far more as a self-employed person than I could working for someone, and I could have the work/life balance that was really important to me. Working full-time on someone else's dream and vision didn't make sense to me anymore.

2. What makes you think you can keep up with big brands?

We're a small content consultancy, so that means we're nimble and can adapt to suit clients' needs and new developments in the marketplace as necessary. We don't have "legacy" challenges, overhead, or "traditional" revenue streams to protect.

For pure strategy we don't need to compete with big brands, such as Contently, that are sourcing hundreds of writers. We'd need investment and infrastructure to do that, and we're not quite there yet. From an event development standpoint, we have the expertise, a growing list of high-caliber speakers, and experience producing everything from intimate dinners to full-scale trade shows with well over 10,000 attendees that I'm betting very few independent companies can offer.

3. How did you frame your digital marketing strategy?

I'm a journalist at heart, so the marketing strategy came from answering the five Ws (who, what, where, when, and why). Who are we? What do we do best? Where do we tell our story? When do we launch? Why should clients choose us?

Figuring out the answers to those questions helped me come up with the company's core mission statement, which led to everything from copy for the website and LinkedIn, to our business cards, to our reasons for pushing back on potential prospects when they think we're charging too much.

4. What is your biggest concern about the success of your business?

Building something that at some point can function independently of me. Right now, I drive the business, including everything from generating leads to closing the deals. I interface with the clients, I work with the team to write copy and program events, and I edit most of our contributors' work. There's no real stepping away from the business yet, but I want to grow a team and develop a system that they can work from that ultimately doesn't require me. That's when it becomes a scalable, viable business and not just an idea that I've convinced some of my friends (and some clients) to believe in.

5. How do you use online marketing to separate you from the rest of the world?

I use two platforms: Written articles on Medium and a podcast called LNCHBRK to interview people and tell great stories about what's happening in the industry. Telling stories on those platforms allows me to shine a light on people I think are thought leaders, which in turn makes those people happy to help promote me and TJK Media. And having other people talk about us is far more effective than talking about the company ourselves.

6. Do you think online marketing lives up to all of its promises?

I'm a huge believer in the power of online marketing when it's done correctly. That means when companies (or entrepreneurs) know the story they want to tell, know who their target audience is, and know which platforms to use to unite those two things.

So if you're a yoga instructor, why did you get into it? What does yoga do for your body, mind, and spirit that brings you back to the mat again and again? What can it do for your students? That's your story, and you tell it on Tumblr and Instagram. For an online real estate listing service—is your software better suited to commercial deals than to residential deals? Is your sales rep getting more inbound leads from commercial brokers? Then that's your target audience, and you use a combination of LinkedIn ads and sponsored content on commercial real estate blogs to reach them.

Online marketing isn't free, it isn't cheap, and it isn't easy, but when it works, it's tremendously effective. It just takes a bit of work to, well, make it work.

7. When you think of throwing in the towel, what brings you back?

Two things. One is that I really, really love this industry. From watching (and critiquing) brand videos on Vine to digging into the latest research on online video consumption (hint: it's all going mobile!) to hitting up industry conferences, I'm quite passionate about digital media and the way it's transforming our lives. So it's that curiosity and desire to learn more and this hunger to share that information and tell great stories about the industry that keeps me going. There's nothing else I'd rather be doing right now, and I think for all the mental stress and anxiety that can come from being an entrepreneur, you have to love what you're doing. You have to get off on it.

The other thing is that I have a really great support system of entrepreneurial friends—so we commiserate and inspire each other—and my family. They cheer me up after I've had a bad meeting with a client and remind me of how powerful I am when I'm scared or even just listen when I need to vent. Support is intangible, but it's invaluable, so it's important to find some people who really do support you.

PROFILES OF DAVID: EUGENE PARK

Meet Eugene Park. Eugene works with Bugaboo International helping to manage its e-commerce and online marketing efforts. Bugaboo describes itself as an International Dutch design company that develops and produces mobility products and is known for its innovative and breakthrough design of strollers. Bugaboo began as a small start-up in 1999 and today employs over 1,000 people, and its products are available in 50 countries worldwide. Eugene and Bugaboo are exactly the kind of Davids we feel privileged to know.

1. Are there times when you feel like you are on a digital marketing island?

Yes and no. I've worked for digital-only software companies where digital marketing was the primary driver for customer acquisition and business growth. On the other hand, working for a multichannel, retail-first brand can result in digital marketing and online initiatives being siloed from other departments. The latter situation can be frustrating but also empowering. Assuming your colleagues are forward-thinking, or at least open-minded, they're likely to take great interest in what you do if you're producing results.

2. What strategies do you use to keep up with bigger budget brands?

Managing big budgets and working within a big brand setting can have inefficiencies. Too many hands in the pot or having too many stakeholders can create bottlenecks in the ability to be agile when it comes to adapting to market changes or optimizing budgets.

Working with a more modest budget requires you to be selective regarding how it's allocated, so my strategy is to have a hands-on role in all online initiatives and to continually optimize my marketing mix based on quantifiable results.

3. How did you frame your digital marketing strategy?

I start by defining goals. Being accountable for delivering business growth requires strict forecasting and an alignment of the marketing budget to meet those goals. I also leave room in my budget for experimentation but am prepared to fail quickly.

4. What is your biggest concern about the success of your line of business?

I can't say that our success brings me any specific concerns, at least not from a market competitor standpoint. I'm willing to bet that our competitors are watching us as closely as we're watching them; however, I/we will continue to innovate and make decisions that are relevant to *our* brand, product, and marketing strategies.

5. How do you use online marketing to separate you from the rest of the world?

I use customer centricity as a key motivator for driving just about all important business decisions whether it is in the formulation of an SEO strategy, retention plan, or e-commerce shipping policy. I also try to avoid "best practices" as much as possible. You really have to figure out for yourself what does or doesn't work well for your online business and what resonates with your audience. Finding your unique formula for success naturally leads to differentiating yourself from the competitors.

6. Do you think online marketing lives up to all of its promises?

At times. Technology is reinventing the way we reach our target audience and is enabling us to communicate with customers in more relevant ways than ever before. On the other hand, there's also more clutter, hype, and misinformation than ever as well—my RSS feed is a good example of that. Finding the right solution partners, vendors, and strategies that make sense for your brand requires diligent research, planning, and testing, but the payoff can be very rewarding.

7. When you think of throwing in the towel, what brings you back?

Ultimately, I'm having fun.

INDEX